LEROY
A TRUE STORY

D. R. MONROE

LEROY © copyright 2014 by D.R. Monroe. All rights reserved. No part of this book may be reproduced in any form whatsoever, by photography or xerography or by any other means, by broadcast or transmission, by translation into any kind of language, nor by recording electronically or otherwise, without permission in writing from the author, except by a reviewer, who may quote brief passages in critical articles or reviews.

Edited by Angela Wiechmann

ISBN 13: 978-1-940014-89-0

Library of Congress Catalog Number: 2013957823

Printed in the United States of America
Third Printing: 2017
20 19 18 17   6 5 4 3

Cover and interior design by James Monroe Design, LLC.

This book is also available in an electronic version.

Wise Ink, Inc.
837 Glenwood Avenue,
Minneapolis, Minnesota 55405

www.wiseinkpub.com
Reseller discounts available.

All for LeRoy

It should be noted that due to the sensitive subject matter discussed in this book, some names, titles and locations have been altered to protect individuals and organizations.

We are sun and moon, dear friend; we are sea and land. It is not our purpose to become each other; it is to recognize each other, to learn to see the other and honor him for what he is: each the other's opposite and complement.

—*Hermann Hesse,* Narcissus and Goldmund

LEROY

There is a man you haven't met, a man you will never meet. Sometimes in the summer, when fresh-cut grass stings my olfactories, I close my eyes, and if I listen as I used to, I can hear his lawn mower coming up from behind. I do not have to step out of the way; I can feel he is still a couple rows to my right. I watch him intimately as he limps by me, pushing the mower with the most excellent precision.

I can see him perfectly. His clothes are dirty, but not because he is. If the mower weren't so rowdy, I would hear the jingling of his mighty key chain swinging maniacally from his khaki belt loop along with his chain wallet—two competing pendulums swinging toward an unknown reward. A cigarette drops from his mouth and onto the shorter half of the kelly green lawn. I watch his damaged, dirt-caked fingers reach down to pick up the smoldering butt. He puts it out in the palm of his hand. It makes me smile because I know it doesn't hurt him. No one else ever knew this but us.

I can only see him in the dark, when my eyes are closed, no matter how many times I try or how hard I concentrate otherwise. Even though I know this will always be true, I cannot help but open my eyes from time to time—just in case the one time I don't, I will miss him.

I was fairly far removed from my time in Wisconsin. In 2004, after completing my undergrad degree in La Crosse, I moved to Santa Fe, New Mexico, to get a degree in the "Great Books," as they called it (although it was more boasting than calling), at St. John's College. I somehow made it through the basic training of Aristotelian arbitration, Bible deconstruction, and *Billy Budd* reformation without getting kicked out and branded an eternal dummy. I came very close, however—I got hit with academic probation my first term. I had to convince two professors to argue my case so I could continue paying $15,000 a year to sit in a circle and defend my "lowbrow sophistication" against misanthropes and hipster trust fund bunnies who pretended to be broken, poor, and thought filled as they pulled into their parking spaces behind the wheels of their BMWs. This was my life for the two years after LeRoy. (I should mention that I define my life by one insistent timeline: BL and AL, or Before LeRoy and After LeRoy.)

After several months of bartending at a swanky club in downtown Santa Fe, the inane hours and after-hours of drinking had caught up with me. It was during Fiestas, the massive paganesque festival of the burning of Old Man Gloom every fall, that I realized I was in over my head.

At the end of the last Fiestas celebration I would ever participate in, I wound up under a large bush on the affluent north side of town near Canyon Road. It was a wakeup call when the aged man who owned the property roused me up and asked me if I knew where I was. It was the first time anyone had ever called me "son." It was especially disconcerting that in order to let me out, the old man had to use a remote to open the seven-foot gate in front of his driveway, a gate that continued around the entire perimeter of his million-dollar home. It took me an hour and a half to walk home that very early morning. I blame it on that confusing realm in which we exist between twenty-one and twenty-five, where we're not quite yet adults and still no longer youths.

Within a couple months of that shit show, I was

hired part-time at an executive capture firm, an opportunity I would have never encountered if it weren't for a fellow student named Keith Woogerd. After a seminar on Nietzsche's *Thus Spake Zarathustra*, he told me the company was looking for grad students. "They are more reliable," he said. "The corporation doesn't have to babysit them as much." I figured this could be true for me, so long as my work hours didn't interfere with my downing mushrooms and whiskey during a century-old festival that involved burning the bad energy out of town through the vehicle of a twenty-foot white-faced effigy named Old Man Gloom.

When I completed the program at St. John's, I moved to Chicago to take a full-time position at the executive capture firm. Chicago was fine. I loved the food and the public transportation. But the job and the noise were not for me. I had to wear a shirt and tie every day. I enjoy wearing a shirt and tie, just not every day. I had only four shirts, five ties, two pairs of slacks, and one dressy pair of shoes. This made it awkward when I sat next to my cubicle mates who had a different shirt-tie-slacks combination every day for two weeks straight. Not to mention the peacoats . . . oh, the peacoats.

I did what I was supposed to do—I didn't ruffle any feathers and, for lack of a better term, succeeded. When I lived in Chicago, four things encompassed my everyday routine: a job I was indifferent about, but was necessary; going to the gym every day in a failed attempt to relive my glory days in Wisconsin when I had been a trophy-winning bodybuilder; reading philosophy; and drinking Pabst and Goldschläger at the basement bar across the street from my apartment, a perfect dive called the Galway Bay.

But none of this was what I was ashamed of. It was the fact that I had forgotten about my life before. It's not that any of it had disappeared, escaped out of my brain forever. I suppose I had just lost sight of what was important. And none of it—whatever it was I was doing—was important. At twenty-four-years-old, I had conjured up my own self-serving philosophy that this was what happened to all of us around this age, that I had to be a victim of this opaque intent during these years of confusion. As I look back, I cannot help but believe this philosophy was born of selfishness and reluctance, nothing more.

My hindsight was not lost forever, although I would have preferred a different reminder. I had a meeting one day, and when I returned from the conference room, my cell phone was flashing its blue light like a finger tapping my eyeball. I can't tell you what that meeting had been about. I can't tell you anything about the day leading up to that goddamn blinking phone light.

It was funny at first, hearing Liz's voice on the other end of the phone. It made me so happy. I hadn't heard her voice in over three years. I didn't even put two and two together, that her calling me out of the blue had to be bad.

"Hey, Dmo. How's old Chicago going? We miss you here," I heard her tell me in the voicemail. It made me instantly nostalgic for a town I had not been back to for far too long. "I just wanted to let you know . . . I'm not sure if you heard or not, but I wanted to touch base with you just to make sure . . . LeRoy died. We read it in the paper yesterday. They had a memorial—not sure about the funeral. Hope you're well. Hopefully see you soon. I'm sorry, Dmo."

It depends on how you look at life, I suppose, as to whether this is where the story begins or where it ends. To be fair, I jump back and forth on this matter myself, regardless of how linearly I am viewing life on that particular day. But today, for argument's sake, for right now, let's say this is where it starts.

To be perfectly candid, most of what happened immediately following that message is a river of sewage. I started crying, so much that I excused myself from my cubicle. Not wanting any of the consultants or associates on the floor to see me, I retreated twenty-six floors below to the main level and then took an escalator down two floors more. I sat in a long corridor that connected our Fidelity building to some other building I had never set foot in.

Keith came down. I had assumed he had seen me crying, trying to escape the twenty-sixth floor like a scared moth trying to escape a moving car. We stayed downstairs for forty minutes or so. I cannot recall what I may have said during that time. Keith knew all about LeRoy—the time I had spent with him, how important he was to me.

A week before Liz left me that message, I had spent my first Thanksgiving without my family. I hosted a feast with my fellow coworkers Keith and Adam as well as my friend Josh and my oldest friend, Carl. I cooked a nineteen-pound turkey, and the first thing we did when we sat down was toast LeRoy. I don't know what compelled me to bring him up to the table of soon-to-be drunkards, but I did. I suppose this is proof he never left me.

I still long to know what I said down there beyond the elevator, if for no other reason than to thank Keith just for being there, for being whatever I needed at that moment, because it is still one of my worst—and I have had more than a few.

I couldn't keep it together. I told Keith I was leaving and asked him to "cover for me." Whatever the hell that meant. (We worked in different departments.) I took the escalator back up to street level and frantically patted myself down for my Parliament Lights. I knew it would be busy out on Michigan Avenue—how could it not be? It was the middle of the day on Michigan Avenue in Chicago. Regardless, I walked out through the revolving doors, pushed myself through the pulsating orbs of unaware people, and heard nothing. I was the only person in the city.

I walked in a daze over the massive field of tile that joined the front of the building to the street, trying to light my cigarette. I knew I was a fucking mess because as I hit the curb, a loud baritone horn knocked me out of my self-absorbed sad fest. All the sounds of the city came crashing back. A large garbage truck rushed past, and the garbage man on the back of the truck yelled at me as it just narrowly avoided ending my life, "Get yo head out yo ass, ya dumb motherfucker!"

At first, I tried to take the bus back to my apartment in Lincoln Park. My false sense of man-strength misled me onto the bus, but before it moved a foot, I tugged hard on the stop cord that hung like a taut laundry line above my head. I escaped just in time, my eyes giving way again as I made my way down the three steps to the street in the only pair of fancy shoes I owned. I wished I weren't such a pussy, I can tell you that much.

I hated spending money on cabs unless I was drunk, but it was the only way I could make it home comfortably. When I got to my apartment, I went straight for the bourbon under my sink. I drank more than half of what was in there as I sat on my bed cross-legged, fishing through the two Tupperware canisters of photos filled with glossy reminders of my time with LeRoy.

I became completely consumed by how LeRoy died. I hoped he had been comfortable. I was angry. I wanted to destroy things. I felt horrible guilt for not being there. I should have been there. I was punched in the chest so hard, I almost couldn't breathe. I felt it should have been someone's duty, someone's sole purpose, to inform me of LeRoy's death the moment he breathed his last breath. I wanted to know who got his horrifically matted cat, Sassy. Where was he buried? Did he die alone? Was he okay? Was he mad at me for not being there? Did he remember who I was at all? How in the hell did he die? And how the fuck did I not know about this sooner?

As I pulled sad sips from my glass, I started to wonder if LeRoy even liked me at all. I thought about the book I had been writing about him for the last two years, cursing myself for not finishing it sooner so LeRoy could have received the praise and attention allotted him. I fell deeper into this guilt, knowing I would not be able to give him half the money I would make off the book, his book, LeRoy's book, if it were ever published, so I could buy him a house—the one goddamn thing I could have given him that no one else could.

I had promised him once out loud when we were having lunch right there in Rosie's diner that I would get him that house. The house that sat forty yards in front of the diner. The house with the huge bush blotting out the front bay window. The house with the front stoop and big yard he could have mowed himself. The house where he could have stood in the driveway and grilled his own mushroom Swiss burgers.

I thought of all these things in a matter of seconds. Years' worth of thoughts rattled all at once like KerPlunk! marbles in my brain. It was impossible to appropriately process what the hell was happening. Then every one of those thoughts came back even more intensely than before. I had never experienced anything like it. I was drowning in pure, undiluted sadness. It fucking sucked.

I came back to the present and turned off the lights—right after pouring a final tall glass of what I thought was good bourbon when I was twenty-four. I drank as much as I could hold in my clammy, shivering mouth. My mouth was cold, entirely freezing.

Exhausted from the stress of the day, I passed out and slept a horribly peaceful sleep, during which I had the most vivid dream-memory of LeRoy. It was not quite even a dream; it was as if I were rewatching a memory of him on a large screen at the once-upon-a-time Jean Cocteau Theater.

I was driving. It was one of the snowy months of winter, and I was picking up LeRoy at one of the bowling alleys in La Crosse. I was running a little late but didn't think about it much as I got out of my Jeep and walked toward the door. I was hungry, and I hoped

LeRoy was ready so I could drop him off quickly and go get some food.

I thought this particular bowling alley was scummy, but LeRoy liked it, and they were nice to him and never gave him any shit about his appearance. That was good enough for me. I walked in and nodded at any one of the nameless faces passing me as I looked for LeRoy's lane. LeRoy liked to bowl down at the end, at lane three or four—usually lane three. I scanned the end aisles and didn't see LeRoy anywhere. Perhaps he was taking a leak. I wandered into the bathroom to do the same, but no LeRoy.

I came back out a little more concerned than before, and a feeling of nervousness-induced nausea slowly replaced my hunger. I walked up and down all the aisles and steps. My once semi-calm inspection became more and more frantic. I was now ill with worry. But then I spotted LeRoy sitting in a chair away from the aisles, not looking quite all right.

I jogged over to him and hunched down in front of his drooping head. "Hey, man, what's wrong?" I asked before my attention wandered primarily to my lingering nausea.

LeRoy raised his head and looked at me. His eyes welled up with tears. It was the closest I had ever seen him to crying.

"What is it?"

"They stole my bag. It's all gone. All of it."

LEROY

The more LeRoy talked, the more upset he became. The tears perching on his eyelids were daring each other to fall over the ledge while he subconsciously tried convincing them not to. I was hypnotized by how the salty blobs just sat there, so close to gravitating to his cheeks, but never rolling down his face. LeRoy wiped his eyes upon noticing the attention I was giving them.

"They . . . they took it. Everything. Everything," he stammered.

"Who did?" My voice was raised, almost cracking, and my concern quickly evolved into anger.

"The kids—they stole my bag."

I told LeRoy to calm down. I put my hand on his shoulder, and I could feel him shaking just slightly, quivering like a stray.

"Some kids—they stole my bag with my balls and my shoes."

I looked down to see LeRoy only in his black holey socks. "Did you see them? Where are they?"

"No. It's all gone. What am I gonna do?" He was quaking.

"How do you know they stole your stuff?"

LeRoy put his head back down and pointed toward a table on the top level near the bar. Two guys, two hickish-looking buffoons, were sitting there, trying not to laugh, but their snickering became unmanageable when they saw LeRoy pointing. I closed my eyes, took a breath, and told LeRoy to sit where he was.

I walked directly up to the table and stood two inches from the face of one of the tall, lumpy rednecks. "Where is it?" I started off as calmly as possible.

"I don't know what you're talking about." He laughed under his tongue.

"You think it's funny, picking on a mentally disabled guy?" This was how I had to speak—there was no use in explaining what organic brain syndrome was or how certain factors can exacerbate it to the point of resembling mental retardation. I puffed out my chest, slightly intimidated by the fact there were two of them.

"Some kids took it. I don't know what you're talking about, kid," he said. The two twits shared a smile in front of me.

"Where's his *fucking bag*?"

The one closest to me stood up, and I immediately grabbed him by his vest and threw him down the three steps behind their table. The other one stood up and took a step toward me. I point-punched him, hitting him hard in the chest, hurting my finger. I told him, "*Don't.*"

LeRoy was now watching. I stood at the top of the steps, still pointing at the other one. "I'll ask you one more time, shithead. Where's the bag? Where is it!"

The manager waddled over to me with a cordless phone off its cradle and informed me he was going to call the cops.

"Wonderful—call the cops. I want you to call the

cops," I dared him. "You have two grown dickheads here that took a mentally disabled man's bowling bag and hid it somewhere because they think it's funny. Call the cops. Call 'em." I held out my hand for the phone, gesturing that if he didn't want to call them, I would be happy to.

The manager just stood there, looking at the short fat one. "What the hell is going on?" The rube just shrugged off the question with a dimwitted look on his craven face. The manager moved his attention to the taller one on the ground. "Bill, what's going on?"

"We're just playing around, Tom," he answered.

I charged down the steps with every intention of beating the piss out of the guy, but Tom interrupted me. "Hey! That is enough!" Tom looked at the two hillbillies. "Tell him where the bag is."

The one not on the ground pointed over to the coat racks. Through a forest of miscellaneous coats and jackets, I could see LeRoy's black-and-red bag leaning against the wall, behind all the apparel. I looked down at the one who had now gotten himself up off the ground. "You're a real piece of shit."

I walked over to LeRoy and asked if he was all right. By now, everyone had gone back to their business, besides Tom and the two shitheads, a triad standing at the top of the stairs. I retrieved LeRoy's bag and brought it over to him. He was nervous but happy to know his most beloved possessions were not in fact lost.

He put his shoes on. "Would you get me an ice-cold Coca-Cola Classic?" he asked.

By now, the two aggravates were finishing their beers and setting up to leave. They never apologized. They never acknowledged LeRoy.

As I headed back, Tom approached me. "You two need to leave. LeRoy's causin' too much trouble. Get out of here."

I whipped around so hard Tom flinched. "Excuse me?" The manager's facial expression faded from confident and pompous to something resembling alarm. "You think I come here to hang out with a fifty-year-old mentally disabled man because I have nothing better to do?"

I still feel bad for saying this. I loved hanging out with LeRoy, but I didn't want Tom to think this was personal. I wanted him to think it was a duty, that I had to uphold an end of a bargain, rather than that he had hurt my buddy's feelings or embarrassed one of my friends. I wanted him to take me dead seriously, and saying those words was the best way I could think to do that as a twenty-one-year old.

"I work for him, sir. I work for him through a government-funded program, a government-funded program that would be more than happy to come in here and find out why you insist on mistreating the mentally disabled. I am also sure they would *love* to see all the fifteen-year-olds in here smoking away and the eighteen-year-olds drinking their Mike's Hard Lemonades. I'm sure they would *love* that. So, sir, I think it would be best if you treated LeRoy with some respect, or I would be more than happy to call my boss right now. Does that make sense to you?"

Tom disconcertedly nodded yes and turned around. Any confidence he may have had was now no longer there.

"Hold on," I barked at Tom. I turned and yelled down to LeRoy, "Hey, do you need anything else?"

LeRoy waved me over, and I complied as quickly as I could. LeRoy leaned in and whispered, "My scores—can you get me my scores?"

"LeRoy would like his scores, please," I shouted in the manager's direction. Tom nodded, no longer such a big, important man. He went back behind the front counter, printed out LeRoy's scores, and walked them back over. LeRoy now felt brave enough to walk over to where I was standing.

"Hold on a minute," Tom said before disappearing behind a plain black door. He came out with a bowling shirt with the alley's name on it. "Here, LeRoy. This is for you. Sorry about all that," Tom apologized to LeRoy, who happily accepted. LeRoy loved that shirt and wore it all the time after that shit day.

About a week or so later, LeRoy went back to the alley for the first time since the incident. I dropped him off at the door, but he called me just moments after I drove away.

"You have to come back. Come back now." He sounded upset.

I whipped the Jeep around and sped back to the alley. I was nervous. Nervous as hell. I thought of those two shit-clamps who gave LeRoy a hard time and immediately felt guilty for leaving him there, for not going in with him and scoping the place out. "Idiot," I said out loud as I ran to the doors, trying not to slip on the ice in the parking lot. Why would I leave him there his first time back? "*Idiot.*"

I sprinted inside and found LeRoy standing right by the front doors. "What's wrong, man?" I asked him, out of breath.

LeRoy was smiling so hard it looked like it hurt.

"What is it?" I asked again.

He pointed to the wall. "Look!" he squeaked.

I looked up and saw the best gift LeRoy could have ever received: there on the wall, engraved on a shiny black plaque listing the 200-average bowlers was the name *LeRoy Buchholz*. LeRoy was an avid bowler and had been going there a very long time, bowling over 200 many times, but they had never put his name up on the wall until now.

I stayed for a while, and we rolled a few games. Tom was more than nice, and LeRoy was back to his old self again. He even ordered a beer and salted it (as he always did) before he drank it down over the course of half an hour. LeRoy did not let the previous week faze him. He did not quit bowling there because he was afraid. He did not want to go somewhere else because of the bullies who had taunted him so unnecessarily. Nope. That was LeRoy Buchholz.

I woke up at 5:00 am, hungover and puffy-faced, thanks to the previous day and night of drinking and crying. I sat on the edge of my bed and fingered the pile of photographs I had tossed through the night before. I came across a Polaroid of a youngish, but not too young, LeRoy in a 1970s white sweater with brown sleeves and a brown stripe across the chest. I stared at the photo for a long while as it became clear what I had to do.

It was the absolute end of November 2006. I called in sick at 6:00 am; scrounged up any cash I had; and packed an overnight bag, a pair of snow boots, and a tent in case I couldn't find a place to stay. I hopped on the Brown Line twenty minutes north to the Lincolnwood suburb, where I rented a space to keep my Jeep for fifty bucks a month—an incredible deal when trying to park one's vehicle anywhere in Chicago. I was driving west to La Crosse and was going to make it to LeRoy's funeral, no matter what.

I grabbed the Brown Line west off Diversey before the sun came up and headed north to Lincolnwood, where my vehicle sat in some guy's parking space. This route was a twenty-five-to-thirty-minute train ride, and it was through the less shitty part of the North Side.

I stepped off at my stop, walked through the super-clean Korean and Vietnamese block of the region, and found my Jeep in its respective parking space, undicked with. Driving out of the city when you are that far north is not much of a headache compared to starting three blocks from the lake. It's nice. It always made me feel as if I weren't in the city.

I was usually spastic when it came to traveling—anal as hell—but thoughts about my final destination must have slipped that disrupting part of me into hibernation. I started to lose track of time when I hit the tollway. I pulled out my Sony recorder, an unexpected gift from Keith, which I stocked with fresh batteries early that morning to capture my thoughts on the drive "home."

I had been working on a book about LeRoy for some time, but by this point in my life, I hadn't yet finished it. I wasn't even close—I just kept writing and adding to it. I think I continued to write as an attempt to rectify my leaving him in the first place, to make the whole experience sound a particular way, to make it last as long as I possibly could. But maybe if I just spoke into this dumb little recorder box as I drove—talking about my time with him, how I felt, what happened—I could write about that. And maybe by the time I finished this necessary trek, that would be it. I pressed the tiny red button with the triangle on it to start.

The surroundings of Illinois—the brown, snowless winter and its biting cold—would eventually morph into the entirely different surroundings of the Mississippi River Valley of Wisconsin. The years rolled back. I was on the creepy merry-go-round from *Something Wicked This Way Comes*, except my time travel wasn't off-putting at all. I wasn't turning into the skeletal remains of a demented ringmaster; I was getting perfectly younger and finding myself back in a time I cherished above all others.

LEROY

I had picked LeRoy up at his apartment one afternoon—he had bocce ball practice. Practice went on as it usually did. Nothing was out of the ordinary, except maybe the heat. It was one hundred degrees outside of the shade. It was July and it was Wisconsin, and although asphyxiating humidity was to be expected, one hundred degrees was pushing it.

As practice ended, LeRoy and I helped clean up the miscellaneous pieces and pack away the equipment into the Special Olympics–branded bags the city of La Crosse provided. The two of us said good-bye to our friends and fellow players and made our way back to the Jeep. But once he got to the door, he realized he had forgotten his coffee thermos—something he never went anywhere without, regardless of temperature. He cursed his forgetfulness in an inaudible string of and headed back to the shade of the large oak tree he had left it under.

LeRoy rushed back to the Jeep at a speed unsafe for him. I shouted at him to slow down. This shrill command from the kid in the Jeep made LeRoy move even faster. He presented an enormous grin that stretched wide across his stubbled face, letting me know he would move as fast or as slow as he damn well pleased. He held the thermos high above his head, as high as he could, as if he had just caught one of the biggest fish he had ever reeled in.

He leaned on the Cherokee, and the two of us

stood in silence for a moment, decompressing from another hot afternoon of bocce ball practice and orange pop. Most days I would take LeRoy back to his place right after practice, but this day I had a different, entirely specific agenda. We headed out for one of LeRoy's staple meals of hot dogs and root beer floats.

We sat on a bench in the parking lot of Rudy's, a great old-timey drive-in that's been in Wisconsin in some form or another since 1933. At that particular moment, it called 10th and La Crosse Streets home. The old orange sign with white letters that screamed "Rudy's" at passersby was perched high above our heads and did nothing to protect us from the sticky hot of the July sun. Our skin, like sponges, soaked the humidity down to our bones; there was no escape. But LeRoy liked the heat, so there was no point in finding relief from it. We sat out in the open while the black asphalt beneath us made the sun feel that much hotter.

LeRoy finished his float immediately, as was his way, and slowly worked on his two hot dogs. One thing fast, one thing slow. On LeRoy's plate you could always find lots of mustard, lots of ketchup, and plenty of mayonnaise—all mixed in one amalgamated orange pond into which he dipped his wiener.

"I want another float," LeRoy said, expecting me to battle him on this request.

"Okay, it's your money," I told him.

LeRoy gave me a perspicacious grin, having been

given an answer he wasn't expecting. "Nah," he said. "I don't want one."

I let the food settle in my belly, allowing the heat to take its toll, before deciding to get on with it. The feeling of ease and confidence I had possessed only moments earlier had now been replaced with an uneasy solicitude. Until that very moment, I hadn't considered that LeRoy could say no. Before, I had just assumed LeRoy wouldn't care—but what if he did? I now felt remarkably unprepared. It's not that I fumbled my words. I had none to fumble. Any words, anything, would have been better than the thundering awkwardness of my silence—nothing for minutes.

Disturbed by my own inability to articulate, I finally just came out with it. "I need to ask you a question. It's *very* important you listen to what I have to say."

LeRoy chewed his dog and stared at me, shooting me a half smile—a taciturn look that succeeded so well at patronizing the shit out of someone. With his mouth nearly full, LeRoy did not break his gaze. Surely humoring me, he simply asked, "What?"

Leaning in LeRoy's direction just slightly more than necessary, I said, "Listen hard."

LeRoy's half smirk faded, and he wiped his mouth with the sweat-and-grass-stained tank top that hung loosely off his torso. He shifted to better view his inquisitor. LeRoy was either nervous of what I was going to say, or he was politely playing along as he thought I was testing his patience. It was most likely the latter.

The life LeRoy had led was too astonishing, too bizarre, and too important for only a few dozen people to have an account of. LeRoy was an incredibly fascinating man, and I wanted to express this to him in a way he would understand. But if I had said just that, he would have dismissed me for using too many words, for being too emotional, too boring, too self-involved.

"You're an enigma," I told him.

LeRoy nodded, pretending he knew what an enigma is. Hell, maybe he did know, but I doubted it and explained it anyway to the uninterested man with a mouthful of hot dog staring at me. I tried to make it perfectly clear he was the most unique person I had ever met.

LeRoy certainly was not one for emotional banter. This particular discourse quickly reminded me of a time when I had given LeRoy a hug. I had just told him some sad news. I thought I had read traces of sadness on LeRoy's face, though I was most likely just projecting my own sadness onto him. I went in and gave him this kind of manly hug, a one-arm-only hug, quick like. But it was a hug nonetheless, and a blind man could have immediately sensed how uncomfortable it made LeRoy. It made me feel stupid. I should have known him better. I let my own shit cloud what was best for the situation, what was best for him.

LeRoy was becoming impatient with me as he

took another bite of his hot dog. As he chewed, he waved the half-eaten food in the air, signaling me to get on with it. So I got on with it.

"Can I write a book about you?" I asked. My voice shook.

LeRoy sat quietly, chewing his food.

I felt I had a responsibility to tell as many people as I could the story of LeRoy Buchholz. I wanted to write a book about the short period of time I had shared in LeRoy's life and what I thought I knew of it, albeit surely I didn't know *that* much.

During this long-winded, self-motivating description of the *why*, LeRoy grabbed one of the seven different lighters he had in his pockets and lit up a cigarette. He took drag after drag off the cheap grit, and another and another. Paying just enough attention to make me believe he was in fact paying attention, he nodded with the Winston still in his mouth, bobbing along with it like one of his orange and yellow fishing bobbers. He said, "Yeah . . . just don't make me look stupid."

3

I was about ninety minutes into my drive when my cell phone rang. I was too pissy and distracted, not to mention hungover, to answer it, but the entire screen lit up with twenty numbers, so I answered out of curiosity. I was completely disoriented by what I was hearing on the other end. My very dear friend Tim, who was doing a tour in Afghanistan, had some phone time and thought he'd give me a try.

It was a serendipitous call. Just hearing Tim's voice calmed me down—just talking to him in general, but also knowing he was okay when I was not. I would certainly never compare what I was dealing with to what he was, but still, it eased my angst. He was in a dangerous place and doing a dangerous job. It may have been the only thing that could make me forget where I was going and why, even if only for the short duration of the call.

Soon he had to let me go—there was a line of fellas waiting to call their girls, their families, their friends. So we said good-bye, and I wished him safety and love. And when I hung up the phone, only a few minutes of physical reality prevailed before I was back in the spot I had been before he rang: thinking of my newly deceased friend and talking to the little black recorder as if it were LeRoy.

Driving from La Crosse, Wisconsin, to Apple Valley, Minnesota, takes exactly two and a half hours door to door. I did not go home a lot during my college years, or at least not as often as some. But I managed to make it home enough so I did not feel terribly alone, so my mother could rest assured I had not changed too much, and so I could remind my family how important they were to me.

The drive was not bad at all, and my favorite part was the drive back to La Crosse from Apple Valley. I would attempt to arrive in the Winona, Minnesota, area around dusk, knowing I would have the best seat to an incredible watercolor sunset over the Mississippi as I rolled down the descending road into Wisconsin. An incredible landscape presents itself down through the bluff valley of the Mississippi River. It becomes quite treacherous to drive because it is so goddamn beautiful it simply cannot be anything less than a gorgeously wonderful distraction.

La Crosse is a picturesque river town over the border, and the descent into it from Winona is a steep one. You are falling down through a huge culvert carved out through the bluffs; you have beautiful rock formations to your right and a deep, seemingly infinite valley to your left. This descent would not be the best place in the world to get into an accident. Then again, LeRoy Buchholz could tell you that.

It had been some time since LeRoy had been home. Between the ages of thirteen and seventeen, he had "run away" in the Tennessee Williams sense from somewhere around Holmen, Wisconsin, one of the several river valleys shadowed by the soft, protecting bluffs. A river valley so green in the summer it seems to be a different color the more you look at it. In the winter, it's cold and white, covered in a melancholy blanket so uninviting, so brutal and cutting, it turns people into outcasts. Thick sheets of hardened water take over the rolling bluffs, almost as if they have to compensate for the brilliant Augusts that precede it every year. These were the familiar surroundings around the home LeRoy had left.

This particular late morning, miles and miles from the yard he played in as a child, he walked on an altitudinous highway that reigned over the river towns of La Crosse and Holmen Wisconsin like Zeus looking down on Athens from Mount Olympus. LeRoy looked much different this day than the day I would meet him some twenty-five years later. No, this day he looked rugged, young, and handsome. He was 80 percent a greaser from a generation he was a decade too late for and 10 percent a "long-haired," as an aging military population had a tendency to call him. The other 10 percent was something entirely different, something slightly odd—a 10 percent that would eventually envelop 100 percent of him.

His hair, shoulder length, was clean, poker straight, and devil black. His face showed a soft black hue that ticked slowly past a five o'clock shadow, still visible even through the heavy rain that fell hard and stung any unprotected skin as if he were walking through a car wash. The rain wore his leather jacket before his eyes, adding character that would be visible to me years later. His jeans were no less dry than the rest of him, and he stood a sturdy and confident five feet ten inches.

LeRoy walked the highway in tough motorcycle boots, although he had never driven or ridden one in his entire life. The rain was reaching Cartagena proportions, and if he had not been so high up on the highway, the water would have swelled up over his boots, soaking his socks and making his trek that much worse. Not that he would ever complain about it to anyone, nor would these conditions hinder him from his journey.

LeRoy rolled a Winston from the right side of his

mouth to the left, using his teeth, not his lips, somehow keeping the cigarette dry—it was the only dry thing for miles. Perhaps LeRoy's tactic of constantly moving the grit created a magical force field of dryness that kept it out of rain's way. Or perhaps LeRoy merely thought constantly moving the grit created a magical force field of dryness. Either way, when it came to LeRoy, this was a plausible certitude.

LeRoy carried a tan canvas soldier bag that was now a heavy taupe due to soaking in relentless rain. Whatever was inside was most likely soaked as well—another circumstance LeRoy could not care less about.

LeRoy was moving southeast on 90, wanting for a ride but not necessarily waiting for one, when a very particular sound perked his astute ears. He was like a dog hearing a high-pitched bird far up in a tree, not knowing exactly where the sound was coming from but knowing it was nearby. It was hard to hear over the incessant sheets of pouring water, but there was a slight distinction between the sound of the rain and the sound of that same rain being torn through and separated by the straight stream of rubber tires. It was a wincing sound only a decibel or two higher than the bullet storm of the rain itself.

LeRoy took the sound as a cue to turn around. Out of some innate response, he extended a dripping leather arm and lifted a thumb up on a hand that had been dirty earlier in the morning but was now cleaned by the weather. A colorless Cadillac boat that took up the entire lane—from the yellow dashes in the middle of the road to the white solid lines to the right of it—passed by him.

The wheeled pontoon slowed down ten feet past the hitching greaser-hippie hybrid. LeRoy looked up, seeing it had stopped to rescue him and pluck him out of the rain as his mother would have done if she had ever come looking for him. He pulled his arm in and put his head down as he ran to the benevolent vehicle.

The environment inside the car would have made a regular human immediately suspicious. You and I would have opened the back door, scanned the interior and the men's faces, thanked them for their generosity, then immediately closed the door, thrown our hoods back on, and stuck it out back in the rain. But not LeRoy. Not necessarily because he was unaware, but quite possibly because he didn't care. Besides not knowing any telltale signs of danger and not having the hammer that would ring that circumscribed bell of caution, he was looking only for transportation.

LeRoy slid across the beaten leather back seat and positioned himself comfortably in the middle. The spot seemed to be missing a seat belt, but with a glance, LeRoy discovered it almost immediately. It was tucked away quietly between the cushions. LeRoy pulled it out barbarically, as if he were trying to tear it from its base. He was rough enough for one of the two up front to shout back, "Easy, guy!"

I don't know what the two men looked like or what they were doing. LeRoy didn't remember much. All I know is a small yet vital piece of information LeRoy shared with me one afternoon in Rudy's parking lot under the hot July sun:

"They were passing a bottle back to each other. Probably booze," LeRoy told me.

Probably booze. No shit, probably booze. For the sake of the story, I am going to say the two men were passing a bottle of bourbon. I don't know why. Let's just say bourbon. Let's just assume cheap bourbon. LeRoy told me one of them offered him a pull from the bottle, an offer he may or may not have taken. Knowing what I know, he most likely declined.

After picking up the faux greaser hipster LeRoy, the car pulled over to the far right side of the road, swung a doughnut, and headed back the way it came. LeRoy didn't care where they were going. He wasn't necessarily trying to get away from anything, but rather just trying to go somewhere else. He knew his chauffeurs were most likely not going to his parent's house, so LeRoy sat tight and enjoyed the dry ride. The two men up front never asked LeRoy his name, and the passenger in the back never asked theirs.

The captain at the helm drove back down the roller coaster path that would lead them into the Mississippi River Valley. The road winds and twists and pikes, demanding the best reflexes from the soberest of drivers. But one can assume this driver felt invincible, thanks to his libations, and most likely thought himself a much better driver drunk than sober. He reached into the back seat, pacing his attention between the front windshield and the roughed-up leather one-seat as he looked for a pack of cigarettes he was certain was there but must have shifted due to the wild rummaging of his newest passenger. As he spent more time looking in the back seat than at the road, they swerved and hit the half-gravel, half-wet soil of the shoulder, which jerked the fool back to full attention. He steadied the Caddy and forgot about the grits for the moment.

On the apex of the highway, they stopped at a truck stop that served ice-cold Wisconsin beers like Miller High Life, Schlitz, and Pabst. As far as I can recall, having driven on this highway dozens of times between the ages of eighteen and twenty-one, this place does not exist anymore.

Once inside and out of the rain, the two from up front sat at small seven-top bar, ordered shots of anonymous spirits, and washed those down with the aforementioned homegrown brews. LeRoy sat at a tiny table behind them. He had ordered a Hamm's he hardly touched outside of shaking salt into it and taking two tiny sips. After some time, the two turned and urged LeRoy to *belly up* next to them, which he did just because.

LEROY

The driver purchased a new pack of brandless cigarettes, forgetting about the pack just minutes earlier he had been certain was in the back seat. The three of them sat at the bar like three monkeys—one who saw no evil, one who heard no evil, and one who spoke no evil—with three shot glasses in front of them and three separate cigarettes in three separate ashtrays. After some time, the driver decided it was time to go, and all three men exited the station and climbed back into their Cadillac—two of them drunk, one of them sober.

Only LeRoy knew, in his own way, how long they were in the bar, and only LeRoy knew how long they drove before the incident, yet he remembered none of it. Out of the blue, the driver remembered there was a pack of cigarettes in the back seat. Not owning up to failure on any level, he made it his personal crusade to rediscover them. While doing so, once again, he began to deviate from the course in front of him.

It happened so fast, the Cadillac was halfway down the gorge before LeRoy even realized it. Any inherent cues LeRoy may have dismissed before were now in full effect, and he was more than aware something terrible was happening. The two drunks had no control over the car hurtling toward sea level, and certainly LeRoy didn't, all the way in the back seat. LeRoy double-checked his seat belt, tugging hard on the strap around his waist, accurately predicting a collision with a boulder at the bottom of the gorge.

The collision was severe. Regardless of LeRoy's preparation, the seat belt snapped like a crisp snow pea, launching LeRoy from the back seat through the windshield while the two responsible rested comfortably in their respective captains' chairs. LeRoy slammed into the rock face like a sack of potatoes thrown at a basketball backboard. The initial impact pushed the Cadillac back some feet as LeRoy introduced himself to the rocky mass. LeRoy slid down the rock mass before the Caddy came back to rest hard against it and, subsequently, on top of LeRoy.

Very little from here has been kept or remembered. Just a few tales of the nefarious gentlemen in the front seat being taken away in an ambulance and LeRoy being left in the pouring rain, pinned between steel and mineral. According to some, he was there twelve hours. According to others, seventy-six hours. And according to still others, longer and shorter measurements of time. But it is not the time frame that matters nor the precise facts of what led to the accident. What is most important is what LeRoy endured.

LeRoy's hip was busted—bad. His left leg was mangled severely. His collarbone was broken, and he had severe head trauma that caused irreversible damage to his brain and nervous system. He also suffered from a collapsed lung. Once LeRoy arrived at the hospital, they did a gastrostomy, which is when they create an artificial, external opening into your stomach for nutritional support.

Even years later, he did not talk about the accident very much at all, especially if pressured to do so. But he did enjoy sharing the part about him telling the doctors they could not amputate his leg. The doctors told LeRoy that if they did not remove his leg, it would be unusable and he would be in a wheelchair for the rest of his life. Nonetheless, LeRoy had them leave the leg, and they had no choice but to do so. LeRoy's identification was not found at the site of the accident; thus, the medical community had no knowledge of guardians.

He said to me, over and over again, "They told me I wouldn't walk," as he slapped his weaker left leg hard with his left hand. "And I'm walking just fine, just fine!"

The doctors could not save the tendon in his right knee, though, nor could they save the fifth toe on his left foot. LeRoy called these *nuthings*. I would ask him, "How do you feel about these injuries, LeRoy? How do you feel about these afflictions?"

"Nuthings," he said. "They're nuthings."

The hospital staff had no choice but to comply with LeRoy's demands. And they were demands, demands that reflected not an attachment to his organic self, but rather a severe understanding of himself as a whole. An odd yet profound sense of ownership of self. An idea of self-extension, perhaps worried that a removal of any part would result in an even lesser representation of an already physically lacking unit.

"You can't have my leg," he told them. "You can't have my leg."

My full bladder began to tug me out of my transitory stopover in La Crosse. Where the hell *was* I? It took me a minute, but it seemed I was a little less than halfway there. I recognized the landmark we all referred to as Window Rock and the signs for the Madison turnoff. I pulled off.

After relieving myself fully and grabbing a bag of cold cheese curds I noticed in an ice cream cooler for the ride, I got back on the highway. It was comforting to know all it took was a full bladder to pull me out of the past with LeRoy and back into the present behind the wheel. At the very least, I probably wasn't running the risk of pissing my pants. And although I felt competent enough to get over the initial barrage of emotions that made it borderline perilous to travel such a long distance, once I was back on the road, it took but a few minutes before I was time traveling again.

LeRoy was one of a handful of children. At one time I was told he had six siblings, and at another time I heard he had twelve. After he died, I would hear even more preposterous numbers climbing all the way up into a Michelle Duggarian realm—eventually reaching as many as sixteen from a Baptist household. There's no proof (or at least none I could ever find) of an exact number of brothers and sisters, but I don't think it matters much at all. No matter how many family members he may or may not have had, once LeRoy left home, no one seemed to be looking for him. He didn't feel he needed to call anyone, or at the very least, didn't feel as if anyone were waiting on a call from him.

It had been some time since LeRoy had been home. During an undisclosed period of time, perhaps in the late 1970s to early '80s, he lived in the forest outskirts of Onalaska, Holmen, and La Crosse—an endless labyrinth of pine and marsh. On more than one occasion, he told me he lived out there for only a year. But on more than one other occasion, he told me he had lived there for three. The last day I saw him as my ward, he told me two years. Like a holy Eastern monk, he lived on food scraps, handouts, and rainwater. But more like a vampire than a monk, he stalked nearby gas stations, waiting to suck vaporous sustenance from his static, mechanical victims. Picture, if you will, this scene that was once described to me.

A Kwik Trip at dusk. Summertime in the Midwest. It's hot and humid from the damp Dairy Belt sun that had been drenching the land all day long. A scraggly looking man with a heavy limp comes out from the tree line smoking a cigarette, like some nicotine-addicted Sasquatch. His name is LeRoy.

LeRoy waits patiently for a car to pull away from a pump with a large white "3" painted on it. He makes sure they filled up a good amount, at least three gallons. Once the car is gone, he creeps up on the nozzle. LeRoy pounces on the metal nozzle, ripping it from its holder while making sure not to pull the release trigger. Now that it is in his hands, he huffs the sweet, oily fumes, devouring the airy meat of the tank's gaseous carcass. LeRoy inhales the substance and sits for a moment on his knees, completely unaware of his surroundings. Everything fades away, and there is just LeRoy, the last man on earth, before his serene existence is interrupted by a fifty-year-old, overweight station attendant yelling from the open door. LeRoy hears the older man over the incessant chiming of the door's alarm. BEENG . . . BEENG . . . BEENG . . .

"Goddammit, son! I'm calling the cops again!"

LeRoy was a huffer, an active participant of inhalant abuse, partaking in the intentional inhalation of chemical vapors to attain a mental high, a euphoric effect. Inhalants produce an effect similar to alcohol intoxication and include symptoms such as drowsiness, lightheadedness, and loss of inhibition. The more one "uses" inhalants, the more one experiences dizziness, hallucinations, delusions, belligerence, and manic apathy. Considering the majority of you went to junior high school, I can assume you know much of this. What you may not know, however, is that long-term exposure to these substances can cause or increase the severity of organic brain syndrome—something else LeRoy had, something else that defined him, something else that demanded his resilience.

Despite the symptoms of these conditions, I did not once witness LeRoy lose any of his inhibitions. This fact is so definitive, there is no other explanation than his inhibitions were not separate from him; he did not have inhibitions in the sense that you or I do. Another example of what separated him from the rest of us.

A semi cut me off, forcing my mind back to the road. I had only been driving half an hour, maybe forty minutes, since my stop near Window Rock. Pumped full of adrenaline from the near miss, my brain stumbled. I blamed the semi, but it very well could have had something to do with the lack of full attention I was giving the road. I told myself I needed to be better about this. It was just getting stupid.

Instead of getting immediately better at the task at hand, my mind worked hard but wandered aimlessly, trying to get back to wherever I had been with LeRoy before all the swerving and braking. I was unable to place it, like when you try to revisit a pleasant dream after waking up in the middle of it. But the harder I looked for it, the farther away it got. Instead, something else was weaseling its way in: these earlier thoughts of LeRoy. And before long, I could not help but think about what started me on the path toward him in the first place.

Growing up I had friends, and first kisses, and second and third-base scores. I was the captain of our high school's cross-country ski team, which was a great experience. I met one of my best friends to this day—Timmy, the aforementioned military man—while cross-country skiing. I was not a football star or the starting pitcher for our oh-so-popular Blaze baseball team, and to be quite honest, I was not the best cross-country skier either. But I was good enough to lead a band of others like me: not the most popular, not the best looking, not the most coordinated, but goddamn, they were awesome human beings. I took after my brother, Jay, it would seem; he too was the captain of the cross-country ski team a full eight years before I tried my hand at it. He was a much better skier than I ever was and did not fall into the unflattering check list of things mentioned earlier.

I didn't love high school, but I didn't hate it either. I went to a couple dances with some pretty good-looking girls with wonderful hearts. I wasn't a cool kid, but I wasn't an outcast either. It was what it was, and it was fine. There was something, though, something special that happened during my last year at Burnsville

High School—something that would turn out to be my first real experience with those like LeRoy.

During my senior year, I started working with students who had various cognitive and physical disabilities. I had shared classrooms with these students and passed them in the halls every day for years. I worked with them in the tall shadow of one of my favorite teachers, a wall of a man by the name of Jon Shelden. I primarily assisted with the athletic aspect of the kids' daily routine, or adaptive physical education. Besides feeling good about the work, I enjoyed it tremendously—it was not as selfless an act as one would expect. No matter how shitty the average day in high school would be, during that one hour Monday through Friday, any resentment or attention toward who was doing what to whom would vanish. That is what I loved most about working with those girls and guys: no matter how you looked or how much you weighed or how badly you smelled, Shelden's students did not care. They did not give one shit about any of that because they were just happy you were spending time with them and they thought of you as their friend—feelings that were easily reciprocated. It was the first time in my life I felt I was making a difference. It was a feeling I connected with and began to crave. I wanted that feeling all the time.

One afternoon I followed Shelden, as I and everyone else called him, into his office at the back of the auxiliary gym where the kids had their class. He was wearing his everyday wardrobe of Nike wind pants with a Nike T-shirt tucked in and his Oakley sunglasses resting on his head.

He sat down in his chair. Every time he sat, it was if the chair disappeared behind and beneath him—all you could see were the wheels. Shelden was a bodybuilder and actually trained me earlier that year in the gym after school. I would eventually go on to win a couple bodybuilding championships under Shelden's tutelage. Shelden swung his large frame around and opened his half-gallon water jug with his molars.

"Danny, if you want to help me out, you gotta want to do this," he told me.

I really did want to help out. For one thing, I was able to get out of some regular classes to help Shelden, and it also counted toward a credit. Shelden looked at me from behind his desk while he tore into a piece of chicken breast he had brought from home, devouring it like a Viking eating to prepare for battle. In between the large bites, he drank from his water jug and prepped a milk shake of the protein variety.

"There is only one thing I can tell you, one thing you need to know to connect with these kids."

I sat on the edge of an uncomfortable metal stool and nodded as a child does to his parent—in a hurried manner, when he wants them to stop talking.

Shelden chewed with one cheek stuffed with

chicken. "It is imperative that you treat these kids like you would your best friend."

I continued to nod like a complete jackass.

"And I'm not talking about being nice or doing stuff for them," he went on.

The instant Shelden finished his sentence, it was quite evident I was not entirely sure what he was getting at. Not wanting to misconstrue or miss out on the genuine meaning of his words, I asked Shelden if he could flesh it out a bit. "I guess I don't know what you mean. So I'm not supposed to be nice to them?"

"Of course you are."

By now Shelden was working on his second chicken breast. He had brought two that particular day. Through his poultry-scented words, he went on, "You give your friends shit. Your friends give you shit, right?"

Again, I nodded unnecessarily. I must admit, at that point I was feeling particularly cool that Shelden was swearing in front of me, as if he trusted me enough or maybe thought of me as one of the "guys" or something silly like that.

My new-found mentor leaned back in his chair, swallowed his food, and went on. "Treat 'em like that. Treat 'em like you'd treat your brother, like your friends, like someone you are comfortable being around. Someone you're not afraid to screw up in front of. You're not here to be flawless, Danny. Nobody is."

Nothing but nods on my end, once again silently thinking I had understood some great, sage advice, some priceless wisdom. I thought I understood what Shelden meant. I thought I knew what it would mean to treat these kids in this way. And regardless of what I thought I knew, it seemed Shelden's main concern was that I not baby them and not act awkward in their presence. I thought Shelden was telling me they did not need to be treated like the "special kids," as so many of us grew up referring to them because it made us feel more politically correct.

After a couple weeks of watching these interactions between Shelden and his students, I thought I was getting "good" at what I was supposed to be getting "good" at. But Shelden's a smart guy. I would eventually come to understand that what he was talking about had nothing to do with getting "good" at anything. Rather, it was about being normal and being yourself—two things that can be a lot harder to be "good" at than one may think.

Andy was one particular student who went to my high school and participated in Shelden's program. To be honest, I had no clue what his actual disabilities were. I think it's fair to say he had some obvious cognitive problems: he had slow learning and slow sentence construction, and he was very anxious, very shy, and very childlike in his demeanor. I should mention Andy was the biggest goddamn human I had ever met as far as weight and height ratios go. The kid was a house. Not just large, although he was overweight, but also tall—like, his nickname should have been "Tiny" tall. When it came to connecting with others, he tried extraordinarily hard. His longing for acceptance made him vulnerable to ridicule. He would trust people not to make him look foolish, but as in every high school, there were those perfidious punks who salivated at the opportunity to exploit this unique trust only the innocent possess. He was a sweetheart, a genuinely kind and compassionate kid who just so happened to also be absolutely gigantic. Think Steinbeck's Lenny without the woman murdering and bunny crushing.

A week after Shelden had his little pep talk with me, there was an issue during class involving this enormous, kind student. To start the day's activities, Shelden would have the students run ten laps around the gym as a warm-up. This seemingly mediocre exercise helped facilitate routine and promote productive skill sets. The gym where they ran their laps was not comparable to a full-court gym. This particular gym, nestled in the northeast wing of the school, was not much of a gym at all. Its technical term was an auxiliary gym. It was more of a big rectangle, really. No basketball hoops, no sidelines—just cement block walls. The space in which these students had to run their laps was about half the perimeter, if not less, than a standard high school gymnasium. So in all fairness, ten laps were not that exhausting. Shelden certainly was not running the kids ragged.

Andy, the aforementioned gentle giant, was like ten foot six, four hundred pounds; a Norseman beast running laps in an area he dwarfed. When he started running his laps, the high school in the next town over could feel the rumble of his long, hard strides. Just these huge *slap, slap, slap, slap* noises with every step, like a lumberjack taking it to a piñon pine, like a giant robotic clown slapping water with his big red shoes.

Shelden was in an administrative meeting, so I was assisting the kids until he came back. I'm talking ten, fifteen minutes at the most I was "in charge." I remember Andy made it about three laps, then he came tromping up to me, looking as though he just ran a half marathon. As Andy approached, I raised my hands up in a *whoa, boy!* manner, as if I were trying to stop a Clydesdale. Andy slowed down, and I shot out a generic "What up, buddy?"

Andy's large frame crouched over the cement floor as if he were trying to see the bottom of an imaginary pond. Not making any eye contact at all, he went on to tell me his legs were burning. He then asked if it would be all right if he sat down until the gang played whatever it was they were going to play that day. Andy half-caught his breath and straightened himself out, stretching like a goddamn Kodiak. I had to strain my neck just to look up at him. Not being anywhere near his stature, I could only imagine the strain running put on a guy Andy's size.

Attempting to make eye contact with him, I said, "Sure, buddy, you can sit out the last seven laps." I used the dismissive, generic pronoun *buddy* once again. Thinking back to what Shelden said, I used this pronoun as some half-assed attempt to make a connection with him. I told Andy to take a seat against the wall and catch his breath, and he plopped on the ground and did just that.

Unexpectedly, my allowing Andy to take a break caused a revolt amongst the other troops.

"Why does Andy get to sit down?" one girl said.

"Why can't we sit down?" another student whined.

"My legs hurt too," one of the quieter kids told me as he tugged on my shirt. On and on like this.

I had never thought I could be intimidated by these kids, but man, I was. So I did the best I could to ease the masses. I decided I too would run the remaining laps, hoping the gesture would relax the unruly crowd I had just created. I played the role of matriarch and reminded them how good they were doing and how beneficial running was, along with a handful of other half-meaningful bullshit remarks.

After a few minutes of all of us running together, Shelden came back from his meeting. "How's everything going?" he asked as his eyes darted around the auxiliary space we occupied. Then Shelden looked at me head-on and immediately asked, "Why is Andy sitting over against the wall?"

I told him the whole story—how Andy's legs were burning and he was really tired.

But Shelden cut me off mid-explanation. "How many laps did he finish?"

"He needed to stop at three," I told him.

"Three laps?" Shelden asked loudly of me, looking in Andy's direction. Andy's attention quickly ran from Shelden's direction to some spot on the ground near his foot.

"Three laps?" he asked again, knowing the answer was yes. Being careful not to curse much in anyone's presence, he said, "What the hell's that all about?"

I straightened up, arching my back as if to make myself appear taller than I was. I looked at Shelden with confidence, really trying to stand by my decision. "Listen, Shelden, he said his legs hurt. And considering how big he is—"

Again, Shelden interrupted me. "Let me tell you something, Danny boy." He collected himself, speaking much calmer now. "Andy hates running, so he is going to say his legs hurt or his back aches or his feet burn or his tummy hurts or any other bullshit excuse so he doesn't have to run laps. They're not stupid, bud."

I immediately felt embarrassed. I certainly did not think they were stupid, and I was always sensitive about how my behavior or my attitude reflected my view of them. I took Shelden's advice to heart—I saw how right he was. These kids were some of the sharpest people around.

As I sulked in my pitiful self-reflection, Shelden made a beeline toward the crafty and victorious grizzly bear sitting in the corner of the gym and staring at his feet. Andy saw Shelden walking toward him, and his eyes got all big, like a Korean drawing of a baby cartoon owl. Andy had that look a dog gets when it goes into the other room, takes a shit on the floor, then comes right back and sits down, peering at you with those guilty eyes that say, "I'm sorry. I just shit in your shoe."

Shelden, over six feet himself, stopped in front of Andy, casting an ominous shadow over the bear. "What's up, big guy?"

Andy informed Shelden his legs hurt and I had said it was okay for him to stop. Shelden nodded calmly and turned around.

Andy followed Shelden like a scolded pup. "Uh, Shelden? What are we doing today?"

Without turning around, Shelden hollered back, "Frisbee golf, bud."

"Can I still play?" Andy asked.

"Of course you can still play," Shelden said, still eerily calm. "Let me grab you a jersey."

He strode back to his office to grab the two jersey bags—old mesh laundry bags, rips and all. Shelden pulled out a light pink jersey, handed it to Andy, then quickly turned around. The teams were always coed, but the girls wore light pink jerseys when they played for the "shirts" team.

Holding the pink mesh shirt, Andy clambered up to him immediately. "Why do I have to wear the pink jersey?"

Eavesdropping on their discourse, I smiled when I heard Shelden's reply: "If you can't run the laps, then you're going to play with the girls."

It's important to understand that in no way was Shelden ragging on the girls or implying the girls were less than. He just knew Andy did not want to wear pink, as no manly man would. Shelden was simply making a point, a point Andy would surely understand, a point that made Andy *want* to run the laps not simply because he had to, but because there were certain rewards for doing so.

Andy looked at the jersey again as if he were making sure it was in fact pink. "I don't want to play with the girls," he said.

"Okay, buddy." (Ha! Shelden used the generic pronoun too!) "Then finish up your laps."

Andy stood up tall, ready to conquer the world. He took the pink jersey, whipped it to the ground (without much effect, as it was too airy to hit heavy on the cement), and let out a loud bear growl.

"LET'S DO THIS!" Andy roared as he went on to run his ass off, finishing the remaining seven laps in record time for any giant Norseman.

This was my first experience with really getting what Shelden was talking about. After that day, I never underestimated anyone with cognitive and behavioral disabilities, and to this day, I remain humbled by their absolute awesomeness. It would certainly benefit the world if there were more Sheldens around and definitely more Andys.

Three months later, I arrived at the University of Wisconsin–La Crosse in the summer of 2000. It was August, and I had never been as excited as I was the day I stepped foot on her campus as a matriculated student.

I remember watching my mother walk across the sidewalk outside of my dorm after we said our goodbyes. My father had his arm around her as she cried quietly, leaving her second born in the unknown arms of college life. I was sad too; my mother and I are very close. I remember feeling guilty for not crying, but I couldn't help it. I was just so thrilled to be there.

College was amazing. My roommate was my best friend, Carl, and we lived together all four years, sans a short stint my senior year when I lived in a Buddhist Center. I made many friends in college, and my first three months of university life made up for all the tormented, depressing, and puberty-miscued years of junior and senior high school. I went to house parties, hooked up with pretty girls, and was introduced to the recreational activity of smoking marijuana. My life was grand, truly, and I would not take one minute of it back for anything in the world.

I started out as a psychology major, as so many young freshmen do. I liked it quite a bit, actually, but what I did not like was that psychology happened to be the second most popular major behind exercise science at the University of Wisconsin–La Crosse. Now, this is not a bad thing per se. But when professors have classes with hundreds of students, they have a maniacal tendency to weed you out by giving massive exams with zero one-on-one time. Students have a tendency to get lost in that sort of crowd, or at least I did anyway.

I understood this more clearly when I received a D on my first test, a D I did not think I deserved yet did not care enough about to argue. I scraped by in my first intro class with a C-. Studying a fascinating individual by the name of Phineas Gage was actually what kept me interested enough to do just enough work not to look like a complete moron to the faculty.

Phineas Gage was a twenty-five-year-old railroad foreman in the mid-1800s. While using a tamping iron to pack explosive powders into a hole in order to cut a railroad bend, the powder detonated. It shot the forty-three-inch, thirteen-pound iron spike into Gage's face, through his brain and out his skull. Although it blinded him, the spike was successfully removed from the frontal lobe of his brain. Life went on as usual—for a while. The one side effect Gage experienced was a full personality 180. The once calm, collected, punctual, and mild-mannered Gage began arriving late to work and appointments, lost his temper quickly, and showed up places drunk and swearing to high heaven.

It's funny how you don't really see red herrings until after the fact. I mean, how else would you know if you saw one? But this certainly qualifies. Traumatic brain injuries have a tendency to cause mental mismatches like Gage's, but this is not their only outcome. I would soon learn brain injuries could affect people in a seemingly endless variety of ways, as it was the case with LeRoy Buchholz.

I was getting closer—making decent time. I checked the recorder; its batteries were still good. I made sure it rested steady on the flat part of my dash above the speedometer. As I passed the soldier-stiff pines that worked effortlessly to keep Wisconsin a sharp green even during winter, my mind was still stuck on those early years of college.

With the exception of that first Psych 101 class, I performed all right in that major and decided to stick with it until my sophomore year. But then on one rushed afternoon while my at-the-time girlfriend was hollering at me to hurry up, I haphazardly registered for a philosophy course instead of sociology for my elective credits. I am completely aware of the cliché

I am about to present, but that first class, Philosophy 101, *changed my life, man*. And it had just as much to do with my first philosophy professor, Kenn Maly, as it did with the initial subject matter.

I loved my first class. In the front of the room, Dr. Maly sat on a large desk. Behind him were two huge white boards. In front of the desk sprawled an ascending tier of 150 seats. The class was half-filled; I sat in the very back. Professor Maly, looking in his mid-fifties, was dressed in khakis and a forest green field shirt. He had longish, curly hair and a full beard. He kicked his legs back and forth, sitting on his hands. He jumped off his desk, startling us all. He started pacing back and forth.

"How many of you drink alcohol?" he asked. Only a dozen or so of us raised our hands before looking at one another for a helpful explanation.

"Come on, my students." He continued, "Who here drinks alcohol? Don't worry, I promise I will not call Mommy and Dad and tell them."

More than half the room raised their hands.

"Okay. That's better. How many of you do drugs? You know, smoke a little dope, hit a little Leary?" Half the room raised their hands again.

"Well, stop it. You kids don't need to do drugs these days. I had to when I was your age because Nixon was president. Only back then did it mean something, so stop it. It's unnecessary."

He continued pacing and stuttering his steps whimsically. I was immediately comfortable in his presence. I had no idea professors could be this way.

The professor went on, getting to his eminent philosophy: "How many of you have been driving—hopefully not after drinking or doing drugs—and seen something ahead of you in the middle of the road?" Professor Maly gasped. "*What is it*? You think it's a dead body. You slow down, getting closer and closer. Now you're certain. Yes! You're certain there is a dead being in the road. Is it a dog? Is it a person? But then you get to the object, and you see it's nothing but a garbage bag. You realize what you see is not what you originally thought you saw!"

He took a moment, saying nothing while he paced. Then he stopped. "This happens to all of us every day. There is always a bag. Everything we think we see, everything we think we know, starts off as one thing and eventually becomes something else—something true. Everything will eventually reveal its true self if we allow it to do so. My purpose over the next sixteen weeks is not to encourage you to regurgitate everything I say, but rather to give you the tools to use those magnificent brains of yours in order to critically examine everything—to see the bag."

This was the first philosophical interaction I ever had. I finished my first course with an A and threw myself into as many philosophy classes as I could.

I learned Ancient Greek (sort of). I went to lectures outside of what was expected of me. I learned Socrates actually never wrote any of the discourses himself; they were instead penned and told in the point of view of his protégé, Plato. I read everything Plato wrote. I read Aristotle, Kant, Hegel, Descartes, and Heidegger.

After a short time, it was as if I were having an affair with the subject of philosophy. I was blowing off parties and drum circles (ugh, I know) to read *The Apology* and skipped dinner with my girlfriend on more than one occasion because I lost track of time while immersed in Schopenhauer's *The World as Will and Representation*. During all of this, my mentor, Kenneth Maly, greatly influenced me. He was a true philosopher. He took me under his wing after a few months of classes and trained me to think like a philosopher—something I would later learn that, yes, most of us have to be trained to do, trained to be. I made philosophy my real and true major in the middle of my sophomore year.

Kenn and I would sit and smoke cigarettes and discuss Heidegger's "Be-ing" and its relation to Hegel. I learned I could actually major in existentialism, metaphysics, and phenomenology. To this day, I blame Kenn for my six years of smoking and snooty disposition toward fancy German beers. I eventually became his teaching assistant, and he even allowed me to teach a few classes while he was in Germany giving lectures on

Martin Heidegger. I learned more in the last three years of college than in the eighteen years that preceded it.

I think what was peculiar to Kenn and my classmates was that I did not fit the mold of philosopher. I was a competing bodybuilder at the time, which did not aid in my peers' ability to take me seriously, let alone assume I had the cognitive capacity to take in and express a subject as dense as philosophy. But Kenn told me once that what made me stand out to him was that I actually tried to make my own conclusions about the world and express serious thoughts encouraged by rather than regurgitated from texts I read. And I didn't simply kiss Kenn's ass by aligning my thoughts and opinions with his. We disagreed as much as we didn't, but somehow it all worked out.

My fellow classmates never took me seriously as I finished logic equations, Good Will Hunting style, in front of a room of fifty people while wearing an Arnold Schwarzenegger T-shirt. Or while I answered deep questions about Nietzsche's true feelings about women—such as his not being a misogynist when so many believed he was—while drinking from a gallon jug of green tea as I munched on Pure Protein bars and chicken breasts I made the night before. But fuck those guys. It was the only time in my life when I truly did not care what anyone thought of me. Unfortunately, somehow that ego of mine, the one that tells me to care about what other people think of me, reared its vexatious head again once I left La Crosse.

So that was me and college. I studied philosophy rigorously in between squats and bench presses. I lived in a shit heap of a house with seven other guys I still love and speak to on a semiregular basis to this day. I fell in love for the first time and was in a relationship that would end terribly and damage my emotional capacity for years. I played Ultimate Frisbee and played pranks on the TKE fraternity house with my roommates because, well, we just didn't like fraternities, and we really didn't like the La Crosse TKEs—such assholes. It was all worth it, every single minute of it. I was a very typical college student loving the hell out of every second of those four years.

However, by my sophomore year, I needed a job. I had been jobless since arriving in La Crosse. "School's your job" was my mother's mantra. She emphasized this for a number of reasons. My parents had saved money for me and Jay so we could go to college and not worry about tuition—something they started when we were little ones. "School's your job" was also repeated to give us no excuse to let our grades slip. School had always been a big deal in the house growing up. Like some Pavlovian response, I took well to the idea of good grades. Good grades equaled happy parents; happy parents equaled no yelling and an easier life. Hence, the reaffirmation of good grades. Don't get the wrong impression—home wasn't too tough. They weren't the Gestapo. My folks were and still are encouraging, loving, and truly thoughtful people. They did not rule with an iron fist. It was more like with a wooden spoon.

So, I was getting above-average grades in college, but I was not supporting myself in any way whatsoever. The lack of a job was really beginning to weigh on me. All my friends had jobs. But my parents really did not want me to work, worrying it would take attention away from my studies.

Eventually, a deal was struck: my folks, in their infinite wisdom, decided I could get a job. This was considered a "deal," mind you, because my folks paid for my school. On many levels, what they said went—or the money did. If my "good boy" above-average grades starting slipping at all, I would have to lose the job.

I don't want to mislead you: my intentions behind getting a job had nothing to do with nobility or responsibility. Like most things during this time in my life, they had to do with women. I wanted to start taking girls out to dinner and down to the bars and to the movies in the hopes it would make me look more attractive as I "wowed" them with pretentious philosophical banter (not knowing at the time this was not in fact a "cool" thing to do). I had no great desire to get a job to change the world, and there were no magnanimous intentions behind any of my pursuits.

I had had a mess of jobs growing up. I had worked as a maintenance and garbage man for the city of Apple

Valley, Minnesota, where I grew up. I loved that job, but I was not sure what that would do for me at school in La Crosse. After all, I had gotten that job through the fateful grace of nepotism (thanks, Jay), and I doubt the experience would have been the same. Besides, it is not with every job that you get to smoke cigars while riding around in a garbage truck, take hour-and-a-half lunches, and go up to the skids to look at porn with half a dozen forty-year-old males during your breaks—which sounds much skeezier now that I write it.

In addition to being a garbage man, I had worked on a farm and as a movie usher at the Burnhaven 8 Theater in Burnsville, which has since been leveled into a parking lot or something. One year, I even solicited credit card applications to mall shoppers during my Christmas break in high school—a job so dolorous, it is incomparable to the others.

Now that I was cleared to get a job in college, I looked through the newspapers and circled any job that caught my eye—anything that provoked my interest. I asked friends and strangers on campus if they worked, and if they worked, for whom. As badly as I wanted a job, I refused to work on campus unless absolutely necessary. After a couple weeks, I had made no progress at all and found myself in the exact spot in which I started. My mind quickly shifted from having to get a job to having to figure out what I would actually enjoy doing.

LEROY

One evening, I was outside in front of our duplex, "The Roadhouse"—called this due to the massive red sign of the same name we had stolen from the theater department's dumpster and nailed to the side of the house. I was sitting on one of the old 1970s airplane chairs my roommate Carl had acquired from a warehouse somewhere in Minnesota. The chairs were a big hit with passersby. They were orange plaid with a middle armrest that had an ashtray, an ashtray that got much use thanks to Kenn's unintentional influence. I sat in the cold fall chill and lit a Prince Albert pipe-tobacco cigar to warm my lungs—my tobacco of choice through most of college. It smelled of vanilla and cherries. And like the smoke from the cigar wafting into the air, a fond memory crept into one of those tiny back rooms of my mind. A memory of Shelden and Andy and those kids I loved working with so much.

After watching me pine over a job for weeks, my roommate Nate came down the stairs at such a speed, it sounded as if he were falling down the steps. He bolted around the corner, huffing his hot breath onto his glasses to clean them and squinting at me through his impaired vision. He leaned up against the wall of our three-little-pigs duplex made of straw. A crudely hung Allman Brothers LP sat crooked above his head. As he cleaned his glasses with the bottom half of his compulsively worn blue tank top, he suggested I apply at a place called CHCS, where he worked.

"How do I not know where you work, dude?" I asked.

Nate shrugged. "Good question. No idea, dude." *Dude* being a pronoun we exhausted for years.

"It's a sweet place to work, dude. They're fantastic. They're actually doing something positive. They're killing it, dude."

Nate discussed the necessary qualifications one must have to work there, which basically consisted of having a clean driving record (because there was a very good chance you would be driving some of your clients around) and not being a dirt bag in general (no history of violence or shady activity like sexual assault or robbing banks). "You know—someone like you, Dmo," he said.

Nate described the format: CHCS had a slew of homes and apartments all over the Coulee region that housed dozens upon dozens of "clients," as they were to be called. Some people stayed at the homes with the clients overnight, and some stayed just during the day. And others would meet their clients where they lived and take them out to run errands, get food, do laundry, attend various activities, and so on. But not everyone did all these things all the time; it depended on whom they put you with, and you would most certainly be working with more than one client at a time. Nate had three, for instance.

I was actually getting a little excited hearing

about this. I became increasingly surprised and a little embarrassed I had no idea this place even existed—not because I thought I should have been omniscient of such a place, but simply because it revealed my nineteen-year-old arrogance. Apparently, Nate had been working there for months.

With one foot on the stairs, he moved as if to ascend the steps, but then he stopped and decided to extrapolate further on his role at CHCS. He paused at the bottom of the stairs and spoke with an intimate grace about one of his clients, a man in a wheelchair with a traumatic brain injury. His name was Antoine. Nate wasn't trying to show off or sound like an impressive, pretentious know-it-all. He was just really good at this stuff. It all sounded wonderful. Then he added one last detail.

"You gotta clean up shit sometimes. Like, human poop. But that's it," Nate said. "Well, that's not 'it' entirely. There's also piss and blood and probably semen in there sometimes," he went on, waving his hands maniacally as if he were magically waving away the words from my brain.

"It's really not that big of a deal at all when you're actually in that situation," he told me. "It's a care job, so the shittiness of it is diminished—so to speak. Task at hand, you know," Nate said as he finally headed back to his den of psychology texts. Nate stayed a psych major but also tacked on a philosophy minor, so we had many wonderful philosophical dialogues over New Glarus Spotted Cow beer and Cali bong rips.

"Task at hand" made sense to me, even without knowing what it fully encompassed. Perhaps it seemed all the more lucid because Nate had said it with a smile. In terms of the nitty-gritty of the job—and there was a shitload of nit and grit—Nate was more professional than anyone I met at CHCS. Nate had that perfect balance of compassion and wisdom, coupled with a great sense of humor. Nate told me, "When it comes to the shit thing, if you think it's embarrassing for you . . . imagine what they're thinking, dude. If they're aware, it probably sucks more for them."

He was absolutely correct. As I contemplated the job, I imagined it could be awkward to carry on with the day's activities after something as personal as crapping and pissing one's pants or giving suppositories. I would come to understand that, yes, it was personal but also a great window to connectivity. It's only awkward if you make it awkward. So that was easy—don't make it awkward. I would later have one client at CHCS to whom I had to give suppositories and then clean up after they took their effect much more quickly than my reaction time. The nervousness that rushed over me was debilitating when this messy and uncomfortable situation arose, but I slowed down and remembered the importance of Nate's words. What had happened there in this client's bedroom that December evening quickly became a nonissue. Experiences like those only disrupt a relationship if you let them.

Heeding Nate's recommendation, I drove down to CHCS in Onalaska, Wisconsin, to apply for a job in person during the fall of 2002. The main office rested quietly in a quaint little building shared with lawyers and your run-of-the-mill chiropractors. Up two tiers of steps that made an L angle M. C. Escher would appreciate was a door with "CHCS" etched in blue on the window.

After opening the door, my first encounter was with Wendy. Wendy was the secretary who greeted me politely with an application. When I went to leave, she asked me to fill it out there in the office, and I obliged. They sent me home upon completion, but it was nice she asked me to stay even that short while. I waited a few days, but no call. I waited a few more, and still no call. So I dialed them, and Wendy once again greeted me. Wendy seemed to remember me immediately and said she was unsure why they had not contacted me. She asked me to come in to meet with the hiring supervisor. After a routine question-and-answer period, they hired me on the spot. It felt great, but then I wondered if perhaps they hired everyone this way, and the specialness quickly faded.

As far as anyone was concerned, nothing sucked more than the training at CHCS. It consisted of roughly a dozen classes, each one lasting anywhere from one to five hours, and we learned everything from washing our hands properly to not using too much bleach when we cleaned the bathrooms seventy times a day. It sucked. We did get CPR certification out of the deal as well as a first aid certification, which pretty much covered them liability wise when it came to the clients. We were paid for the training hours—a nice perk, but probably expected by most.

There was so much to learn in order to correctly handle the clients and prepare for the very real chance of something dramatic or dangerous occurring. There are so many different types of individuals at CHCS: nonverbals; biters; self-abusers; severe APD (antisocial personality disorder) cases; and people with Down's syndrome, cerebral palsy, and pica.

Learning about pica was fascinating. It was one of two things that kept me from nodding off during those mandatory, hours-long gatherings. This four-letter little devil is an eating disorder typically defined (I'll let the DSM-IV handle this one) as such:

The persistent eating of nonnutritive substances for a period of at least 1 month at an age in which this behavior is developmentally inappropriate (e.g., >18-24 mo). The definition occasionally is broadened to include the mouthing of nonnutritive substances. Individuals presenting with pica have been reported to mouth and/or ingest a wide variety of nonfood substances, including, but not limited to, clay, dirt, sand, stones, pebbles, hair, feces,

LEROY

lead, laundry starch, vinyl gloves, plastic, pencil erasers, ice, fingernails, paper, paint chips, coal, chalk, wood, plaster, light bulbs, needles, string, cigarette butts, wire, and burnt matches.

Imagine holding the hand of a forty-three-year old who then rips away from your grip to go munch on some cigarette butts. Or there you are, walking along, and BAM! He's on the floor ingesting loose change like Takeru "The Tsunami" Kobayashi at a hot dog eating contest. And of course, the first thing that comes to your mind is, "Holy shit—this guy is eating change!" Imagine having such an uncontrollable drive to eat loose change, like an obsessive compulsive who washes her hands exactly nine times every time the doorbell rings or has to open the fridge five times when she walks into the kitchen. The mind is a mysterious fig.

The other thing that kept me from getting sleepy was the woman who led the trainings—Jolene. Besides having a superb and bubbly personality only made stronger by the font of knowledge she possessed, she was very good-looking. Her family owned a bar in northern Wisconsin, where she also worked from time to time—this only adding to her already-jam-packed cache of awesomeness. I thought her classically pretty. I was under the impression she had a boyfriend of sorts, so I had to admire her from a safe distance—in the least creepy sense I can convey.

At our first training, Jolene said, "Okay, you

guys—we have a lot to cover. But we have quite a few sessions to cover it, so don't sweat it. I like to start the first session with questions. Do any of you have questions you want to ask right away?"

A woman raised her hand sheepishly. Her nametag said "Barb."

"So. . . I know this sounds silly, but what do we call the people we work with?"

"By their names," Jolene answered. "You call these people by their names. It's a great question to start with. Although the individuals—or clients, as we call them here—do have a range of cognitive disabilities, they're people and they have names and we call them by their names. When describing their various disabilities however, those with autism are *autistic*, and those with Down's syndrome are *Down's*. And I'm sure we all know *retarded* is unacceptable. *Mentally retarded* is acceptable when dealing with someone who is, in fact, mentally retarded. However, I, as well as many others, find it to be more than acceptable to refer to these individuals as *MRs*."

The heart of the training, though, was to emotionally prepare us for the work ahead. Jolene told us, "Anything can happen at any time. Be prepared—you may be forced out of your comfort zone."

Her words came to fruition quite quickly. Before long, I was at a CHCS house, sitting on a couch, sandwiched by two MRs. Five others were lying on the floor, slumber-party style, watching *Finding Nemo*. One client stood up, calmly walked to the television, and pulled it crashing to the floor.

Jolene also warned, "You all at some point or another will witness some disturbing things—things that may affect you." This was also true. I once rushed to find a client bashing his head on the rim of a bathtub. His face was bloodied, and he didn't seem to know where he was.

Here's the bottom line: the training was necessary and integral. But once I started working, I could tell some employees had slept right through it—which was unfortunate for both them and the clients. So much of the training came down to trust. A great deal of trust comes into play in any profession that deals with helping those who cannot help themselves. For the organization itself, it's a double-edged sword: you can't function successfully as a company if you don't trust people enough to work for you. Instead, you can only try your best to hire those you hope can be trusted. Fortunately, the great majority of employees I worked with were truly wonderful people. I found most to be compassionate and perfectly sweet, and they had genuine probity in their work.

As Jolene said at our last class, "Look, what it comes down to is that these are people like you and me. And I don't mean in an 'everyone's the same color' kind of way. I know its cliché, but guys, it's so important to realize this. It's a relationship, and the sooner you realize this, the easier it will be."

7

I looked at the little green numbers on the clock in the middle of my dashboard, which told me it was a little after eleven. I wished I were there already, but it wasn't far now—a couple hours.

Still, I thought one more time how I wished I were there already. I began to worry, or think so hard I thought I was worrying: I didn't even know where LeRoy's funeral would be or whom I should contact about it. Shit, I didn't even know if I had missed it already.

Why had I been so hasty in leaving? It was as if I had heard the world was ending, and I just jumped into my car and drove north without getting any details. Certainly I could have contacted at least a couple people to find out one or two details. It was idiotic to go about it this way. But now, the numbers I needed in order to find out what the hell was going on were sitting somewhere in a plastic tub under my bed back in Chicago.

It had been only a couple days since he died. I was sure the funeral hadn't happened yet. Confident in my knowledge of completely unknowable things, I picked the recorder off the dash and held it in my right hand to get a closer, hopefully cleaner sound. I stopped to make sure it was picking up everything clearly. It was. I cleared my throat and spoke into my little black memory machine, planning to leave enough recording space to fill in the last details I would collect during his funeral.

Before LeRoy there was Antoine, my first client at CHCS. I was sitting at a table almost too small to function as one. I tapped my heels rapidly on the carpeted floor in JB's office. JB was short and perfectly Midwestern. She had dark hair, she dressed in work-casual clothes, and her top lip curled just enough to notice when she spoke. We were going over Antoine's books together. I scanned medical records, family histories, financial balances, fitness and emotional goals, grocery lists, laundry schedules, and so on.

While I sat there with my legs crossed, intently studying it all, JB slowly raised her head just enough to give me a glance from her brows creeping up just above the rim of her glasses. "Keep Antoine's books in order as best you can," she said.

This seemed like a *duh* thing to say, but whatever.

She put her pen down and positioned herself in such a way that demanded my full attention. She took her glasses off. "Really."

I nodded quickly and nervously, uncrossing and recrossing my legs. "Of course," I said. "I'll do my best."

It took a minute before the gravity of the responsibility sank in. I panicked. You see, this was a problem for me. I can't—and I mean *fucking cannot*—balance my own checkbook, let alone take care of someone else's. In this case, that of a wheelchair-bound, brain-damaged adult man named Antoine. As I continued to cross and uncross my legs at a ridiculous tempo, I started running through numerous silly and emotionally dramatic scenarios in my head.

She could see right through me. I knew it. I could feel her staring into my brain, straight through my dura matter, using her experience of dealing with idiots like me to see through my lies and incapability—my filthy, stinking incapability. I shouldn't have even been there. I was certain I would ruin this man's finances—unintentionally, of course, but ruin nonetheless. I was sweating now.

I began to form excuses and explanations in my head, already preparing how to describe to JB months from now that I had lost all of Antoine's money. I envisioned Antoine homeless, begging for money on Pearl Street in his wheelchair because some dumbshit kid couldn't balance his checkbook. "I'm so sorry, Antoine. I didn't mean to ruin your life," I'd tell him, putting a five-dollar bill in his empty Styrofoam cup as he sat in the cold out front of the coffee shop.

My heart beat harder and faster. I was definitely sweating through my clothes. Suddenly my internal rants were interrupted by the squeezing of my wrist. It was JB.

"It's really simple, hon," she said, trying to break through my neurosis.

I looked up, a little embarrassed when I realized how heavily I'd been breathing, and I saw once again those reassuring corners of JB's mouth turned upward, smiling me down ever so harmlessly.

She let go of my wrist, and my mind settled a bit. "Trust me," she said. "I'm confident you won't screw any of this up."

I liked JB. She was like a mother. With no error, she played the role of friendly boss. I always knew where I stood with her. She had none of that superfluous, apathetic air a lot of bosses have, where you never know how to act because sometimes they are really relaxed and your pal and other times they are raging asses. JB had none of those confusing qualities. She made me comfortable. She helped me relax and taught me how to trust myself in uncomfortable situations when dealing with clients.

JB proceeded to teach me how to record Antoine's finances. There was a form in the back of his book—the big binder of records and files for each client. The form was set up as a grid of columns and rows. In the left column, I was to write what Antoine purchased for food and drink, where he purchased it, and how much it cost. In the row, I was to record the date and the restaurant name. In the column on the right, there would be a running tally of Antoine's available balance. Record a meal; subtract the amount from the available balance. Make a deposit in his bank account; add the amount to the balance.

It really was some of the simplest math a job could ever require. However, I would find ways to fuck it up. This became apparent the days I received calls from JB in between my classes.

"Dan, Antoine's books are short four dollars. Fix it!" she'd shout nicely, like a cattle-calling mother warning her children dinner was ready.

Most times, it was not that detrimental, really. Sometimes I'd just temporarily make the math come out right by adding my own money to his account—a short-term fix right before the books were audited. But eventually, I got a call from JB that reinforced my earlier fears from that first day learning how to balance his checkbook. "Dan, you need to come to the office as soon as you are out of class."

I never went to the office to deal with client matters, so when JB asked me to come in, I knew it was not to chat about the news or who Paris Hilton was hj-ing that week. I arrived at the office in Onalaska, headed up the steps, and marched pass Wendy's desk. She looked at me without threat, but the look indicated she probably thought I was a bit of an idiot. I wasn't offended by this; to be fair, her assumptions were not entirely incorrect. I passed two smaller offices and walked to the room at the end of the hall—JB's office. The door was ajar, and she lifted her head and gave me a fake smile that was meant to be recognized as such. I was terrified.

JB said, "Antoine's books are off by sixty-three dollars."

Sixty-three dollars! I felt sick. I now assumed she called me in to fire me. I was positive she was going to fire me. Why wouldn't she? I flat-out could not account for sixty-three dollars of a client's money. That was not a small amount, especially for these particular individuals, and it was definitely more than I could afford to "fix" myself.

I had one job: protect the clients and their cash. It appeared I couldn't even do that. My breathing increased and became heavy with each exhalalation. My nerves were tight, and my ears were flushed red, almost purple (something that happens to me when I get nervous). As JB opened her mouth to speak, I closed my eyes and wrenched back, preparing for a hard verbal punch reaffirming my failures.

But there was no impact, no words of umbrage, no yelling, and ultimately no firing. They had not fired me the first time these accounting problems had happened, or the second, or the third. They were not going to fire me this time. Every time I had discrepancies in my client's books, it would be cleared up. JB would always give me a chance to fix my errors.

I took the books home that night and went over every entry for the month. (We employees turned the books in at the end of every month so JB and other managers could look them over for errors, such as a swing of sixty-three dollars.) Each time I had to fix such a problem, it was tedious as hell for sure and could take up to three hours to do it. But shit, it was better than mathematically destroying a client's financial records and subsequently my job.

I always found where I screwed up. They were always mistakes in my addition and subtraction—simple-ass math. And no matter how many times it happened, I was always shocked. I could not understand how I could completely shit all over the simplest of arithmetic.

But CHCS was an understanding group. They were very forgiving and trusting, and I was grateful for this. It wasn't that CHCS trusted me because they had no choice. It wasn't trust for trust's sake. I think they understood I was not taking money from Antoine. This had meaning because a small number of employees did in fact steal money from the very people they were supposed to be watching out for, supposed to be protecting from those who so easily preyed upon them.

8

Man, I really shouldn't have left without contacting anyone. I didn't even know what I'd do when I got there. I didn't even know where I was going to stay, for Christ's sake. I thought about going to the Buddhist center first to say hi. I knew they would let me stay. I did, after all, occupy a room there at one time.

I still had some friends in town, but there was no way they still lived where they had four years earlier. And showing up out of the blue to ask for a place to crash seemed a bit dickish, so I scratched that idea. If I were honest, the last thing I wanted to do when I arrived was see anybody, talk to anybody. The only person I felt like talking to was the very person I could never talk to again.

Maybe I'd go to Rosie's. Rosie's was, after all, the safest place I knew in La Crosse. It was the only place LeRoy and I could go to escape from everything—from everybody. I could find haven there again. Who knows—maybe they'd even remember me, maybe they knew about LeRoy dying, maybe they would know some details. Regardless of all the maybes, one thing was certain: I could definitely get a mushroom Swiss burger and a cup of coffee.

I watched the road ahead of me disappear at a straight line in the gray sky. It looked as if it might start snowing soon. I hadn't even bothered checking the weather before I left. As I thought about people I still knew in La Crosse, I came back to Antoine—another person I had lost focus of during all of this scrambling to get back. Between the thoughts of snow, I began to connect some similarities between LeRoy and Antoine I had never really made before, the most blatant one being their preferred choices in dining: LeRoy at Rosie's and Antoine at Menucci's.

One snowy afternoon in January, I was attempting to get Antoine up and ready for the day. The short lamp on his desk did almost nothing to illuminate his small living space, which consisted of a dresser, an old computer, a bed, and a piss jug he used when he could not make it to the bathroom or when no one could help him to it.

I liked Antoine. I sensed he felt ambiguous toward

me, but ambiguity was better than antipathy. I often found his story a lugubrious one. It seemed unfair. Antoine had been in a motorcycle accident some years ago when he was in the navy. He had a wife and children—a nuclear family that slowly disintegrated in the years after his accident.

I got Antoine out of the prone position underneath his bed covers, and together we worked hard to get him out of bed and into his chair. I pushed him up to his desk, where he signed on to his online gaming website and proceed to peck at the keys. With his right hand wrapped tightly in a weightlifting glove and his left hand shaking, he aligned different-colored shapes to score points and win prize money he could use to purchase gifts like Ghirardelli chocolate and espresso makers. After losing too many times to be considered acceptable, he shifted his torso almost completely around to face me in lieu of moving his chair one inch.

"I was in the navy," he said.

Antoine had a salt-and-pepper beard that would go weeks without upkeep, and he looked at me with one eye that lazily tried to focus on my face. The other eye was covered with an old nylon eye patch. Every other week, he would switch the patch to the other eye, thinking it would make his sight that much more acute—something it did not in fact do. This particular afternoon, the patch obscured the view of his right eye, his better eye.

"I was in a motorcycle accident, yah know. I mean, that's kind of how I got here." His voice sounded a lot like Brad Pitt's in *Kalifornia*, but deeper and with a little less drawl.

"I had heard something about that," I said.

I was still a novice with Antoine—with all of CHCS, really—and I had not quite gotten a handle on him yet.

Antoine went on to describe that he had been riding his motorcycle on the navy base, where he was stationed. "I was tearing ass on the asphalt with my woman on the back," he told me as his whole body shook as if he were working a jackhammer. He did not remember how he lost control of the bike. He said his wife had walked away with a broken arm or a broken collarbone—he could not remember which. But that was the extent of her injuries.

"I forget quite which one she broke. Maybe both. Aw, shit. I don't remember. But it was definitely one of those," he said. With each word, he got angrier that he could not remember.

Antoine's injuries, however, were much more severe than his wife's. He suffered broken bones, but his helmetless head took the brunt of the impact. Antoine could not recall many of the details from right before or after the accident. I never pressed him—or anyone else, for that matter. I felt it was an invasion of his privacy. It would be a little bizarre and voyeuristic to know exactly what had happened if Antoine did not even know. I would later encounter hearsay that Antoine had been drinking the day of the accident, but I never saw any proof of this, and Antoine never mentioned it, so I left it alone.

Antoine was obsessed with games—you know, sweepstake-type stuff, giveaways. If Pepsi or McDonald's was running one of their games like Pepsi's Billion Dollar Sweepstakes or Monopoly, Antoine was all over it. So when McDonald's was running their Monopoly game, I would take Antoine through the drive-thru, where he would habitually order a milkshake and large fries—just enough to get his game pieces.

Nate and I did our very best to discourage this colossal waste of money. We just knew there were better things on which he could spend what little money he had. But it was difficult to change his mind because he was so intrigued by these deals, so sure he was gonna win "this time." He'd get so goddamn excited. You can be sure Antoine is still spending the majority of his disposable income on those traps and lottery tickets.

Wednesday night was pizza night. I loaded Antoine into the front seat and put his chair in the trunk. We drove down to Menucci's Pizzeria on 4th and La Crosse Streets, directly across from campus. Antoine liked it there very much. Mostly, I think, because John and Marilyn, the owners and cooks, knew his order by heart: an eight-inch sausage-and-mushroom thin-crust pizza with water and/or a Pepsi with no ice. (I put ice in his cup once, and it was kind of an ordeal.) John and Marilyn treated Antoine with more respect than anyone else I had ever seen interact with him. If I believed in heaven, John and Marilyn would definitely be going. They'd be up there, John flinging angelic pizza dough, and Marilyn braiding Jesus's hair, telling him what a wonderful man he is. They charged Antoine only a buck seventy-five for his pizza and give him his drink for free. This was significantly less than the real cost. Antoine never asked for a discount; they just gave him one.

Once a week, John, who was a pretty decent cook outside the culinary realm of pizza, would whip up something extra special for Antoine. It was always homemade—something John and Marilyn would prepare for themselves to eat at home. Their house sat right behind the restaurant, nearly connected to it. One week it would be casserole ("hot dish" to those in the Midwest). The next week venison. Then mostaccioli, duck he had shot the weekend before in Janesville, beef Stroganoff, spaghetti and bear meatballs, chicken and turkey pot pies, sturgeon and northern pike. Antoine was never charged for these meals.

John and Marilyn would join Antoine and me from time to time when there wasn't a long line at the order counter. And when they finished their long, sometimes hilarious, sometimes philosophical, sometimes educational, and sometimes depressing discourse over supper, all I could do was fill in $1.75 on the left side of Antoine's books. John and Marilyn were Antoine's friends. Antoine believed this for sure, which was important because Antoine was no longer able to inspire himself. He needed people like John and Marilyn to do it for him. They even invited Antoine over for Thanksgiving dinner every year to feast with their own family, welcoming Antoine to be a part of it himself.

John and Marilyn meant a lot to Antoine and to CHCS. To everyone else, they were the grumpy husband-and-wife team behind Menucci's Pizzeria. The first, second, or even fifth time you went in, they may not have come off as hospitable (if you caught them on a bad day) or at all jovial, caked with flour and stained with gunshot wounds of marinara. Their gruff attitudes and disheveled looks were a result of long days in the kitchen, but they had a near-perfect recipe for generosity and Midwestern nice.

Having been in the military, Antoine spent some time at the VA hospital in Tomah, Wisconsin, roughly a forty-five minute drive from La Crosse. The way he talked about his time there led me to believe he would have much rather been back there than in that chilly, dark bedroom in La Crosse. This made sense. Perhaps at the VA, Antoine was reminded that he was once a part of something greater than himself—a collective group of like-minded individuals. Antoine's feelings about the navy felt romantic on some level, like a mistress he wanted to keep satisfied, that he wanted to go back to.

Whenever he had enough money, I would take him to the military base outside Tomah. Antoine used his military ID to shop at the PX store. I don't know what it was about that store, but he thought it was the greatest goddamn place he had access to. Everything was much cheaper than in other stores, which Antoine liked a lot. But it also seemed to bring him back to an environment that never felt foreign to him. He would talk to the officers and talk about the navy with me, stalling in order to spend as much time there as possible. He would buy me a rod of Rolos and a bag of beef jerky, no matter how much I insisted he not spend any of his money on me. Antoine was happiest there at the PX. Toward the end of our time together, I tried to get him to the PX as much as possible—if for no other reason than assuming whoever took over next would not do so.

Antoine told me he had also been in another accident. He was being transported to or from the VA when another vehicle struck the van, causing it to roll over completely. I was never really sure when this accident had happened. Antoine had little memory of it, and no one else had information about it or otherwise wanted to talk about it. So it became yet another mystery surrounding Antoine and his current physical condition.

LEROY

It seemed the VA accident had played a larger role than the first accident when it came to his functionality from the waist down. Antoine would be wheelchair bound from then on out, but not paraplegic. And as Antoine said, "It kept my dick from working."

"You still got quite a libido there, though, Antoine," I said, patting him on the shin, right above where his ankle supports ended. He really did, always asking women how they were doing, telling them how beautiful they were, and on some occasions sneaking in a kiss on the top of their hands after going in for a shake. Every so often, there would be a kind girl who wasn't entirely freaked out by his innocent and harmless advances.

"Yeah, well, I'm not dead, but a lot of good that does me," he said. His chin slowly slid around from his shoulder to the center of his chest and stopped there. Antoine shut his one strained and self-improving eye in defeat.

The entire room seemed to get darker than ever before—the silence unbearably heavy and the air tangible with tragedy. As Antoine sat there, silent and sad, I had no idea what to say. It was the first time I knew I had absolutely nothing in my arsenal to make him feel any better. It was also the first time I felt like crying in the presence of a CHCS client. It would not be the last.

I would be in La Crosse by twelve thirty. I wondered if my ex, Machelle, still lived there. The idea of staying with her crossed my mind and lingered only ten seconds. Our relationship spanned most of the period I knew LeRoy. But even so, neither of them brought up memories of the other. She met LeRoy only once, and I think he had made her uncomfortable.

Part of me still wanted to call up Mac and see her. I suppose I figured it would make me feel better, which was doubtful in reality. She may have taken my mind off LeRoy for a while, but what good would that have done? The last thing I needed was my focus off LeRoy. It was probably a good thing I didn't have her number.

But just thinking of her quickly brought me back to my time in Lax.

The phone rang midmorning at some ignorable hour during me and my roommates' High Life-induced slumber. It was the end of February sometime. It was JB on the other end, and she asked me in that hurried voice of hers if I wanted to work with a new client. I paused for a bit and contemplated the idea. I wondered, would I still be with Antoine, or would she make me dump him and focus primarily on this new person? And if they did put me with some new guy, would Antoine be upset? Would I be able to see him at all? Would we still have Menucci's Wednesdays and our existential talks in his bedroom? Who was this new client? Would he or she like me as much as Antoine did, and if not, did I have to stay with that client? I realized I didn't really know the rules in this area. Luckily for my sake, my neurosis was interrupted by the voice on the other end.

"Hon, I'm not really *asking* you. You're going to be working with a new client."

I said nothing, knowing she was just going to continue talking regardless.

"He's a piece of cake. The two of you will get along just fine."

In the quickest way verbally possible, JB informed me that the guy currently spending time with this soon-to-be new client of mine had recently revealed himself to be a fairly shady character. In not so many words, JB suggested she suspected this guy—I'll call him Dumbshit—had been skimming money from this client. An accusation not to be taken lightly. She gave me no details, and I asked for none.

JB informed me the new client's name was LeRoy Buchholz, and he was forty-eight years old. He mowed lawns in the summer and worked various maintenance jobs, including cleaning CHCS's main office in Onalaska—things for which he was paid. JB told me to come to the Onalaska office sometime that day to discuss LeRoy's case and see if all the "pieces fit."

When it came to matching employees with clients, CHCS was meticulous in making sure the two people involved lined up with one another: social with social, quiet with quiet, complex with particular. JB wanted to be absolutely positive this transition would work for me and for LeRoy. This particular case was very important to JB for reasons I would discover later.

"Come in today, and I can brief you on LeRoy's history—it's a long one," JB said.

I got off the phone and headed out to my porch. Our house—which was haunted by the ghost of an elderly woman who died in the basement in a bizarre bathing accident—was an old, comfortable little two-story with four bedrooms and both a front and back porch. The front porch was off limits to smoking due to the presence of Matt's snake, Minos—a common Greek reference from numerous mythos, including *The*

Iliad and *The Odyssey*. But more specifically in this case, the name referred to the snake-tailed gentleman in Dante's *Inferno* who sat at the entrance to the second circle, the beginning of proper Hell, and doled out rightful punishments.

Out of us four roommates, I was the only one who smoked cigarettes daily, so I was religated to the back porch. Although cramped, it was glassed in and had wooden floors—it seemed an appropriate place to smoke. I went out back, sat down, and lit a cigarette.

I let out a drag and watched the smoke while I wondered if this potential new client of mine was a smoker. I didn't know any CHCS clients who smoked. Up until that point, I had only known one client personally—Antoine. I didn't know whether clients were even allowed the habit. If that were the case, I wondered why CHCS would not allow their clients to smoke, which led to more thoughts of smoking. I rode that thought-train for a few stops and got off at the 1950s, thinking about how you used to be able to smoke anywhere: planes, churches, universities. I started to think about myself—how it seemed, at times, I was born in the wrong era for my complete and most advantageous liking. Smoking in class. How much I would enjoy smoking in seminars. Discussing Kant, Hume, and Nietzsche—how these individuals would be perfectly complimented with an extended-filter Parliament grit resting between my fingers. The smoke's many tentacles interlocking with the smoke from all the other students' cigarettes smoldering next to mine.

My mind, so far off, finally meandered its way back along the smoky thoughts from four cigarettes ago. I came back to what started this internal tangent: a Mr. LeRoy Buchholz. *I can brief you on LeRoy's history—it's a long one.* I replayed those words in my head a few times, those last words JB said.

A little while later, I was driving down Highway 16, the main road in La Crosse. It was really the only highway in town. It led to the exit for the Onalaska office. But instead of the road ahead of me, I could only concentrate on this LeRoy character.

I had actually heard of LeRoy once or twice prior to JB's call. I was almost positive I had seen him once before, riding this beast of a red adult-sized trike (or his "bike" as he and therefore I simply called it, eschewing semantics) through campus. In my initial reaction, I found LeRoy a little odd. But then again, I suppose most people did. As I drove down 16, I pondered how LeRoy must be pretty high functioning if he worked for CHCS, mowed lawns, painted. I was intrigued.

I flicked on my left turn signal and pulled up to the stoplight nestled between the Valley View Mall and Pier 1 Imports. The busy intersection's multifarious distractions did nothing to pull me out of my deep LeRoy thought, until a loud car horn blasted through my open passenger window. I flinched, causing my thoughts to shift from LeRoy Buchholz to how much I hated this fucking intersection. The damn light took forever, and there was always at least one loquacious cell phone chatty prattling away, missing the green arrow, raising a hand in that sorry-I'm-such-a-huge-ass way. I guess it was me playing that role now.

The light turned green, and I drove onward to 52 and exited on Sand Lake Road. Onalaska—a small town with Christmas banners hanging across Main Street during December and a Fire Muster in July—was just north of La Crosse, roughly the distance of French Island end to end. This is where CHCS's western regional office is located. I pulled onto the freshly tarred driveway and took a lofty whiff. That smell signified the beginning of summer to me, even though it was not even yet springtime. I stepped out of the Jeep, put out my cigarette, and made my way across the slightly tacky tar.

I noticed a familiar car and spotted Randy waiting patiently in the passenger seat. Randy, a middle-aged client with what seemed to be severe autism plus something else I was sure I did not know, sat with his seatbelt on, even though the car was not idling and was in fact turned off with no keys in the ignition. Randy was playing with his hands. It looked as if he were using some sort of crude sign language. He was drooling slightly, enough to leave a slug-like trace on Josh's arm rest. I snuck up on Randy's side and slowly slid my hand up the window like Minos climbing his plastic tree, moving back and forth, back and forth, until I got Randy's attention. I raised my head up the window just enough to expose the top of my hairline at first, then my forehead, then my eyes. When my eyes met Randy's, I shouted, "RANDOOOOO!"

Randy yelled out some unintelligible noises and smiled a huge smile—a smile that looked like it hurt. Doing so signaled to Randy that he'd been drooling, and he quickly wiped his mouth with his sleeveless forearm. His noises slowly faded as his attention closed in on the fact that this person staring at him through the window was Dan. Dan was a grownup (kind of). And grownups have money (sometimes).

Randy slapped his hands together, palm to palm sideways with his fingers facing opposite directions. He grunted, still smacking his hands together, all the while smiling ear to ear. I translated this inherent body and verbal language of Randy to mean, *give me money*.

I shook my head. "Rando, I ain't got no money for you, brother." I pulled my pockets inside out.

Randy lost interest after he deciphered this to mean defeat—no money for Randy today, at least not from Dan.

I made my way through the front doors to CHCS's office, which at the time shared space with a chiropractic business with the oddest hours I had ever seen. I always thought it was some sort of a front, some sort of laundry for sure. I never saw anyone in there. The building also housed some low-cost lawyer trio with catchy names like Swetty, Hymen, and Lutz—one of those concoctions you see during noontime commercial breaks for heroin-like court shows.

I started up the steps, passing Jolene's training room. I wondered if her being nice to me lately was just that, or if she found me attractive, or if she had some sort of interest in me—you know, to date. Right then, Jolene leaned out of her office, bracing against the doorframe with her shoulder.

"You going out tonight, dork?" she asked.

Startled and very happy to have this interaction, I told her I was not.

"You have an overnight somewhere at one of the houses?" An overnight was when employees stayed the night at one of the dozen or so houses where CHCS clients lived.

"Nah, I'm not going out tonight. Well, kind of. I mean, I bounce at Brothers a few nights a week."

Brothers is a bar in downtown La Crosse where I worked as a bouncer and barback for about a year—a job I really enjoyed. Jolene made a face that sort of taunted my job as a bouncer, and I just smiled and nodded, reaffirming her silly gesture and pretty face. In all honesty, I loved that she thought it was dumb, and it made me like her that much more.

It was quiet for a moment. Right before it

reached awkward, I grunted, "Yeah, well. . ." making it *completely* awkward. Good job, me.

She nodded a little, simply to be polite, I imagine. The awkward silence picked up right where it left off. Finally she said goodbye. I went to nod a goodbye and realized I had never actually stopped nodding in the first place. I felt like a jackass.

I immediately erased this from my memory and continued on my route, heading up the steps, taking two at a time. I opened the door quietly and was greeted by Wendy's feverish typing. She was always typing with her Winnie the Pooh paraphernalia surrounding her like a tiny plastic audience. On her desk sat a picture of her, a girl I assumed was her daughter, and a man I assumed was her husband, with a dog I assumed was her dog.

"Hey, Wendy," I said. "Whatcha doing?"

"Filing, always filing. Thank God it's Friday," she responded.

"It's Monday."

"Shit," she whispered with a smile.

Walking down to JB's office, it hit me that I hadn't thought about LeRoy in the last twenty minutes or so. My mind had switched off in the car at that intersection, and I hadn't thought of him since. Now I felt completely unprepared.

I knocked on JB's half-open door, and she waved me in, smiling and rolling her eyes at whomever she was talking to. (She was constantly on the phone.) She covered the mouthpiece and whisper-shouted, "Candy—eat that candy."

There was a bowl of candies on a little end table next to her desk. None of the table could be seen, as it was covered in papers and folders of multiple colors. I looked around the office and then back at the bowl. JB gave me a don't-be-such-a-pussy face, and I reluctantly submitted to her demand—in part. I grabbed a piece but couldn't go as far as to put it in my mouth. I'm weird about eating food out of public receptacles.

In the meantime, JB went back to the conversation I had walked in on. "Yes, I know how he gets. However, if he wishes to pee his pants because he thinks it's funny, you still need to attempt to keep him from doing so."

I smiled and laughed under my breath. I enjoyed walking in on these conversations. I played a game where I tried to piece together what they were discussing while doing my best to jump into the conversation, an uninvited three's company. I mouthed the name *Josh*. JB shook her head with a no that taciturnly told me to quit interrupting and playing my annoying game. I guess it wasn't Josh.

JB hung up the phone and looked at me as if she were trying to remember why she wanted to see me in the first place.

"How's Antoine doing?" she asked, still trying to

remember the reason for my presence.

"Antoine is doing well," I told her, not lying. "But he has been a little cantankerous lately. He gets annoyed and frustrated when he's unable to do certain physical tasks."

She nodded and agreed. This had been the norm for a long time now and was certainly understandable, considering his present situation

"I should take him to the Y again soon," I said.

I had started taking Antoine to the local YMCA and was getting pretty decent results from it. Antoine loved working out; he told me he really got into lifting weights when he was in the military. I pushed him to get out of the chair and off his walker, which was encouraged when clients went to the Y. I would support Antoine on his left side, holding him up only so he wouldn't fall, and let him shuffle his feet as we moved from station to station. It took longer to get through the evening, but the results were definitely worth it—actually walking from machine to machine.

At first, I thought it was my idea to bring him to the Y. But in retrospect, it was Nate's idea. I am fairly certain Nate brought Antoine there before I did, and I only brought him there upon Antoine's suggestion because that's what he and Nate had done. Regardless, it built Antoine's confidence and reversed the strong atrophy of his leg muscles.

Music to her ears. JB was very pleased by this,

regardless of whose idea it was. "Is Antoine taking to it?" she asked.

"Well, at first he didn't like it at all. He almost refused to keep going because it more or less highlighted his weaknesses. But I told him we all start out somewhere, and we're all usually weaker than we would like to be. But that's why we keep coming back—to outdo ourselves."

I sounded like a self-help guru. I hated the words, even though they were true. There was a noticeable peak in Antoine's confidence level, which climbed each time we went to the Y. Now it was the first thing he asked about the second I walked through the door.

I was sure, though, this had more than a little bit to do with the staff at the Y. There were more than a few pretty young women Antoine enjoyed flirting with on a regular basis. His favorites: the seemingly attractive middle-aged woman who worked the front desk and called him Tony sweetly as she patted his gloved hands; the one or two college girls who walked the floor of the gym, wiping down equipment, flashing them dimes at Antoine as they passed, innocently inserting themselves into the dreams he would have about them later that night; and the occasional Wisconsin soccer mom who toned her arms and ass for the pool boy or still-interested husband. But shit, if that got Antoine to the gym, then so be it.

JB was pleased by his attendance and the rising

confidence. This was a very good thing for an aging, broken man whose wounds brought on by beating himself up far outweighed those brought on by motorcycle and VA transport accidents. He was a good man and deserved to feel like one.

JB paused and stutter-spoke before sitting down and shuffling through a few folders. I was used to these thoughtful interruptions by now and bided my time at the tiny cluttered table where the remaining candy sat in its dish, uneaten, getting stale. She repositioned herself physically and mentally.

"So, LeRoy," she said, tossing down a folder titled "LeRoy" that looked like a flat autumn cornucopia full of various papers sticking out.

"So what's the deal with this LeRoy character?" I asked her. I was immediately embarrassed for using the word *character*.

"I'm getting there, hon," she nicely snapped. "Do you mind working with him? I mean, I think I want you working with him. Dumbshit is working with him now," she said. It should be noted that JB used his actual name, but for confidentiality reasons, "Dumbshit" seems most fitting as a replacement. "I don't think I like him. He seems sneaky, and I think he might be stealing from LeRoy. I'm not sure, but I don't like the feeling. And I don't think LeRoy is crazy about him either."

"Shit." Realizing I just said *shit* in front of my

sweet, mild-mannered boss, I lost my train of thought. But either she didn't notice or she didn't seem to give a shit about the bad language.

"You'd be surprised, hon. We've fired people in the past for stealing from the clients. It doesn't happen very often, but it does happen."

JB told me there were only a few things I needed to do when working with LeRoy. LeRoy lived on his own, rather than at a CHCS home. He paid his own rent on an apartment downtown. The more she explained, the more it seemed I wouldn't really be working at all—I would be more or less just hanging out with the guy.

"LeRoy cleans the office every Friday around noon or so. Whenever he wants, but not too late," she told me. "LeRoy mows about a dozen lawns—at each of the group homes. He does this on a rotating cycle. Or if one grows uncontrollably, they'll call you or Rob—don't worry, you'll meet Rob—to let you know. Then you and LeRoy can tackle that one first. You know, if you need to mix up the rotation. Each lawn takes him anywhere from one to three hours. But Rob will tell you more about that later."

Once again, I displayed my horrifying habit of monotonous nodding as she informed me LeRoy would also see if any little tasks needed to be handled at the houses, he'd take care of said task, and then he'd mow. Or he'd mow and then take care of tasks. It made no difference what order he chose, and it was entirely up to him.

It seemed LeRoy had complete, free rein. I had trouble thinking what LeRoy would need from me, really, besides a ride. I asked JB bluntly, "So, what is it you need me to do exactly?"

"He needs a ride," she said.

In my mind, I saw a blurry reflection of a strange-looking man in a sweat-stained tank top, back facing me, pedaling away on his bike as I drove my Jeep along Pearl Street in downtown La Crosse.

"He also needs you to pour gas from the gas can into the lawn mower."

Now, why would he need help pouring gasoline? I felt a bit timid, and due to some misplaced sense of naïveté, I did not ask why LeRoy needed assistance with the gas. I would come to learn how important it was to always ask why—always, no matter what.

I was cautious when it came to most of the proceedings at CHCS. The most plausible reason was the overwhelming need I felt to respect these people's privacy. I felt some things were probably best kept unsaid. I thought most of the details of these individuals' lives were, frankly, none of my goddamn business. There had to be *some* secrets about these people that could remain in the dark. Why not? We all have our secrets—embarrassing, troubling, shitty, elating things we do not want others to know about us. Skeletons hang in everyone's closets; most of us are able to keep them there. So why did these individuals have to pull theirs out just because I helped them buy groceries or helped them get dressed or helped them open a checking account? There are things about all of us we wish were hidden even from ourselves, let alone from others. What about our position, besides the mere idea of it, gave us permission to pry into our clients' lives? Why did they get the shades pulled away from their secret windows, only for us to gawk with mouths agape, judging, cringing, and gasping? I thought this voyeurism to be unfair at best, and even though I should have asked certain questions, I chose not to.

At any rate, I guess I believed I was protecting LeRoy in some way by not asking more details. Outside of simple curiosity, I genuinely did not want to know why LeRoy could not pour gasoline. One might imagine I kept my mouth shut out of pusillanimous reasons. Perhaps I didn't want to learn something horrifying. Maybe LeRoy had been badly burnt. Maybe some assholes lit him on fire or made him light himself on fire. Maybe he was some result of a fraternity initiation or a victim of a random act of violence. Truthfully, I had never seen LeRoy's face, a face I now imagined to be scarred by deep cracks of burns. My vision of LeRoy went from Harvey Dent to Two-Face in an instant. That had to be it, I thought. He must have been taunted and abused. Yes, taunted then burned, that was it for sure. The thought of it made me uncomfortable and pissed off, and I completely forgot what we were just talking about.

JB cut through this silent, tangential rant and revealed the details I had chosen not to ask about. "LeRoy used to huff gasoline," she said.

JB must have noticed some change in my face—a look of disbelief—because she smiled again. The explanation was so completely opposite of what I had expected to hear. It hadn't been a gang initiation or some soulless act of hate. I mean, I had been watching *Faces of Death* in my mind for the last ninety seconds. It was a substance abuse problem, plain and simple. I knew what huffing was, of course. I had seen the commercials on TV telling us impressionable youths that huffing can kill you the first time you do it. I even knew a kid in junior high who huffed the aerosol residue from whipped cream cans to get high. For underage kids, it was easier to get than booze, I guess, but huffing always seemed like a lot of work to me.

Now, it's important to explain LeRoy's background a bit as it relates to his issues with huffing. Some of this information JB told me that day in her office; other pieces I would learn or pick up as time went on. Some were nothing more than rumors and theories. One should know that the details pertaining to LeRoy's past were sometimes pieced together by multiple people or were missing chunks of information altogether.

LeRoy had been one of a bunch of siblings

—somewhere in the high single digits or low teens. It seemed, by the words of some, that perhaps LeRoy's father wasn't the nicest or noblest of men. This was not an exact truth to be known. LeRoy never spoke of his father to me and never directly alluded to any suspicious behavior that may have taken place by his father's hand. He spoke only of his mother.

In 2007, years after I left, a woman came forward to say LeRoy had been in foster care with her, possibly when he was about thirteen. No one at CHCS had known about him being in foster care. Beth, a fantastically thoughtful woman with a particularly large role in CHCS's day-to-day operations, had had an idea, a feeling, that maybe LeRoy had been a foster child. Beth was a boisterous woman with a heart of gold and a pleasant eccentricity that could only be matched by her benevolence. Beth had hunches a lot, and these hunches were usually dead-on.

I heard one theory that after being in foster care, LeRoy went back with his mother and then ran away sometime after that. When he took off on his own, he was huffing gasoline and getting high on a regular basis. Some have speculated (most likely not incorrectly) that a matter with one of his family members (most certainly not his mother) instigated LeRoy's huffing. Perhaps he had been forced to do it as a punishment, or maybe it was some sadistic act of cruelty for no reason. Perhaps Mr. Buchholz just did it with his son as some bizarre act of bonding. Sometime after working with LeRoy, I heard a rumor that someone in his family had asphyxiated him in gasoline until he lost consciousness and then resuscitated him. But like many of the stories that echoed off the halls of CHCS and its houses, this was never proven. One must take these with a grain a salt, but perhaps not entirely dismiss them altogether.

Regardless of its origins, LeRoy's habitual huffing contributed to his persistent brain damage and subsequent organic brain syndrome. LeRoy huffed gas for quite a long time and had gotten picked up at a gas station for just hanging around, trying to get some fumes through osmosis.

Which brought us back to our present predicament: what do you do if someone has a job mowing lawns yet is supposed to keep a good ten feet away from gasoline at all times (according to a rumored ancient court order)? That's where I came in.

JB told me LeRoy would never think to start up again with all that huffing. "He more than knows it's bad for him now and doesn't want anything to do with it. I told him not to, and ever since, he's never even attempted to get one last taste."

She went on to explain that LeRoy lived on his own, rather than at a CHCS home. He paid his own rent on an apartment downtown.

So there it was—this mysterious story of LeRoy the lawn mower. I was quite amazed that LeRoy was trusted to mow the lawns regardless of his gasoline-saturated past. I thought of this man's family life, being brought into this world with no burnt offerings and a slower mind than most, the possibility of abuse, his brain damage, the gas huffing, and the lawn mowing—all of it in some way or another interconnected. The heaviness of it all. This guy—how could he handle this past that had been so discomfuckingbobulated? On top of all of this, he was still resilient enough to have all the things he had, like his own place, and to do all the things he did, like mow lawns.

I thought to myself, but still said out loud, "This guy is one badass cat."

"Sweetie, you have no idea."

Pacing back and forth like a general belting out strategies, JB continued to relay on the ins and outs of LeRoy Buchholz.

"He gets paid every Monday, Wednesday, Friday. Fifteen dollars on Wednesday, and ten on Monday and Friday. He gets reimbursed for purchases, if they are legitimate."

In a way I had never been looked at before, JB's eyes scanned mine comfortably, making sure the confused young man sitting at the familiar little table in her office was okay, that he was following along. "LeRoy has his own money, so he can spend it on whatever he wants," she said, continuing.

He had special privileges not extended to other

clients, but this was due to him functioning on a much higher level than any of the others. Like all clients, LeRoy received an allowance for designated purchases such as groceries, medications, and laundry, but he also earned his own money from his two jobs and could spend that as he wished. For purchases with his own money, he was reimbursed only for essentials: food, aspirin, Band-Aids, bills, and so on. Stuff he did not get money back for were things such as lottery tickets, extra packs of smokes, lighters, etc.

"Pay attention to LeRoy's purchases," she warned. The corners of her mouth curled slightly as she tried to keep her professionalism. "He once tried giving Rob a receipt for tampons."

Apparently, LeRoy did not always work out the details when devising his quick scams and money-making schemes. Rob validated the story some time later. LeRoy had found the receipt on the ground, and having no idea what tampons were, he tried getting reimbursed for them.

JB gave me LeRoy's financial records, medical history, and a bio in no particular order and with large timespans missing. All of these things were kept in a beat-up, torn-cornered, blue three-ring binder that looked as old as LeRoy and would be forever referred to as his *books*.

Something else I learned: LeRoy had very specific, albeit bizarre, eating habits. LeRoy was allowed to smoke too. A lot. He sucked down about two or three packs a day. He could use his allowance on extra packs if his weekly allotted cartons were to run out (although this rarely happened). I would find there was a lot to learn about LeRoy, but none of it was hard to master. He was so habitual in his routines, everything was fine once you learned them.

JB sat down and placed her hands on her desk, spreading her fingers like Chinese fans unevenly atop the usual clutter of papers and three-ringed binders. She lifted her head slowly and looked right through my face to the back of my skull, making me a little uncomfortable.

She sighed and said, "Oh yeah . . . and never, ever eat a goddamn thing he cooks himself."

I was so close now. The lines of forests standing at attention on one side of the highway and the farms rolling on the other had been burned into my memory as much as my own childhood backyard. I knew I would soon be passing the first real house off the highway through West Salem before I reached the outskirts of La Crosse. It was easily recognizable due to its massive one-acre front lawn.

LeRoy was mowing a lawn on 22nd Street in La Crosse the first time I saw him face to face and not in the reflection of my rearview mirror. After my meeting with JB, I had some idea of what to expect, but my lack of total knowing excited my nerves and wrenched my bowels. (I have a tendency to be a nervous shitter, depending on the gravity of the situation.) I needed a nervous bathroom break.

JB had mentioned something about LeRoy, something I thought about as I prepared for my first encounter with the man. She gave me a kind of warning that LeRoy might do something shocking in my presence the first time I met him, like a test of some kind. The more I thought about it, the less concerned I was. In reality, I had already seen some pretty crazy shit since working at CHCS. The chance of seeing something more shocking was doubtful.

I pulled up across the street from a very sleek Victorian house flanked by what seemed to be hundreds of short green bushes that embraced the entire house like sandbags surrounding the large green yard of a lake. I jumped out of the Jeep, not knowing how warm it was thanks to the only-feet-apart oak trees lining the street and draping a blanket of shade over me. I rushed up the sidewalk steps with an alacrity clearly brought on by my excitement and anticipation.

A gray chain-link fence wrapped around the entire front, left, and right sides of the house and met a large wooden horizontal-plank fence in the backyard. As I walked through the gate, I was greeted by a portly fellow with curly black hair. He was sweating in a gray, ill-fitting sweat suit, getting everything he needed out of it. My greeter was Dumbshit.

"Hey, Dan," he said excitedly, approaching me as

if we were the very best of friends.

"Hey, Dumbshit," I said with zero inflection.

Dumbshit certainly considered me a friend, and my awareness of this left a strange, though not all-consuming, guilt that covered my tongue with a film whenever I spoke ill of him or at him at all. It was difficult because I had known him before CHCS and initially did not think he was that bad of a guy. He was personable, seemed polite enough—perhaps almost too polite at times, as if it were false. But I now had a near severe distaste for this almost perfectly round person. When it came down to it, I thought Dumbshit was genuinely a good guy before JB told me the secret accusations of his shady doings at CHCS. He immediately went from this seemingly nice guy to this shady, shifty, untrustworthy guy and remained so even as he stood in the backyard sweating profusely, chewing on a Slim Jim. (Did I mention he was sweating?)

Dumbshit moved his big body in my direction, a sort of slow lurch. "So you're taking over for me, are ya? JB put me with a new client. Apparently they need me really bad."

It's a strange position to be in, knowing the truth about someone when he is completely oblivious to the real situation. I nodded and smiled, patting Dumbshit on his sweaty shoulder. "Sounds good, man."

While attempting to avoid looking directly at Dumbshit, I caught a glimpse of a man straggling over in our vicinity, but it was apparent this man was not heading directly toward us. I seemed to be of no interest to the man; he clearly had something else on his mind. This individual had an extreme limp. It immediately reminded me of a zombie from some George Romero film. He walked as if he had been shot in the leg and felt no pain, yet his leg was dying, having gone weeks without treatment, and the rest of the body was compensating.

He wore a white tank that was downright filthy. It was tucked into a presentable pair of light khaki pants. The knees were slightly worn out, and the ankle cuffs were in the process of turning completely green from a decade of lawn mowing. Around his waist jingled two huge chains that crisscrossed in the back in a cumbersome way. Attached to these chains was what appeared to be a set of a thousand keys. He could certainly never sneak up on anyone in this condition.

He wore a pair of spectacles covered by a second pair of gas station sunglasses. The lower half of his face was covered by shaggy salt-and-pepper scruff, longer than a five-o'clock shadow. His hair was greasy but not dirty. It was dyed black, but a small patch of gray appeared toward the back of his skull. His skin had the coloring of a Mexican field worker—it looked like tough, worn leather but somehow did not age him. He wore a monastic pair of white tennis shoes darkly stained halfway down with the acute green of

LEROY

Wisconsin's summer grass.

Around his neck lay four necklaces. The first, the longest of the four, fell all the way down his concave chest; it was the Star of David. (I would later learn the man was not in fact Jewish, nor was he religious in any way.) Under this was a plain old silver chain. On top of that was a white Hawaiian puka-shell-and-rock necklace I had seen on every frat boy douche and *Real World* cast member since 1997. This particular pebbled necklace acted as a choker. Not purposefully—it was just too small for the man's neck. Finally, there rested a pink-and-purple little thing he seemed to have retrieved from one of those little bubble vending machines at the grocery store, near the front automatic doors.

This man was LeRoy Buchholz.

LeRoy's scam hound leaned in real close to me, his chin acting as a conduit for sweat leaking all over my left shoulder. He whispered, "I think he's Jewish."

Dumbshit got the attention of LeRoy, the limping man, and began to talk slowly, as if he were speaking to a baby.

"LeRoy . . . this is Dan," he said in slow motion.

"Hey," LeRoy said to me without making eye contact.

LeRoy kept his head down as he walked past. He was neither excited nor flustered, but not entirely uninterested either.

"How yah doing, buddy?" I asked, regretting as

soon as it came out of my mouth that generic term I had not used since Shelden's classes. I was immediately annoyed with myself.

"Fine," he said with almost complete ambiguity.

Not looking at anyone in particular, LeRoy barked into the air, "Mower needs gas."

Dumbshit wobbled over toward the dilapidated garage to get the gas can. The garage looked as if it could collapse at any minute. LeRoy and I held the silence until one of the live-in workers at the 22nd Street house interrupted to tell us a nail was sticking out of the wooden fence in the backyard. She asked if I had a hammer, because she could not find the one they kept at the house. Being a maintenance man myself at one time, I had a toolbox in the hatch of the Jeep. I left the yard, running to get my toolbox. I grabbed it and jogged back. As I made it to the fence, I suddenly stopped short when I heard a huge commotion.

"LeRoy! Don't! No! Dammit!"

I now hurried my stride to a quicker pace. Dumbshit was yelling at LeRoy—not loud, but more like a scolding tone toward a child. Dumbshit, the live-in, and another girl my age who worked at the house were all huddled around LeRoy. I maneuvered my body and neck a few times, lurching and crooking to find the best angle, but I could not see around the live-in woman and Dumbshit's gray obstruction of a body.

At last, I saw LeRoy leaning up against the fence,

acting cool and calm, patting his torso and chest for what one could only assume were his cigarettes. Without finding or caring about his cigarettes for the moment, LeRoy popped off the fence with a rigid rise and held his wrist outward with the palm facing up, far from his body. The fleshy part under the thumb joint was torn up, and he was bleeding, running down over his palm and tracing the outline of the veins that rose boldly from his forearm.

LeRoy slowly lifted his head, and the straighter his head became, the bigger his grin got. Now smiling hard, he said to the live-in, "*Uhp*, better call the ambulance." He limped away quickly, just ever-so slightly looking back, checking for our reactions.

A bit older than LeRoy himself, the live-in was an older woman, who, like most of them, was so goddamn nice. She smiled gently as she took over the task of holding LeRoy's wrist. She put her head on his shoulder and sighed his name. The woman left him leaning up against the house sweetly, like a fragile package not to be handled too roughly, and sprinted as much as she could into the house. She returned with a tall brown bottle of hydrogen peroxide, Q-tips, cotton balls, and the such. She cleaned his wound while LeRoy flinched and made loud seething noises every time she touched his hand—noises that were returned with a jovial, "Stop it, you big baby." The live-in covered the hole in LeRoy's palm with a Band-Aid, and they exchanged a sweetness of looks. He thanked her by staring at her and looking away, and she told him he was welcome with a similar glance.

As it turned out, LeRoy had heard the live-in mention that there was a protruding nail in the fence and that she needed a hammer. The persistent yet hammerless LeRoy attempted to drive the nail into the fence using the palm of his hand. As a huge surprise to LeRoy, his hand wasn't stronger than the nail. Rock beats scissors.

A little embarrassed from all the attention, LeRoy wandered back to the lawn mower, now filled with gas thanks to Dumbshit. LeRoy started up the mower and finished cutting the grass. It was then that I remembered JB's warning I had earlier dismissed. What I had just witnessed—LeRoy grinding up his hand, using it as a hammering device—was in fact a bit shocking. But I would eventually learn this was not the most shocking thing LeRoy Buchholz would do in my presence.

11

I was done sitting in the car. I mean, I still had a little ways to go yet, but mentally, physically—my ass—was done sitting in the car. The closer I got to downtown La Crosse, the more I felt drawn to LeRoy's apartment. Not in a mystical way or anything like that, but it was strange. I knew he wouldn't be there, so why go? If I closed my eyes, I could see flashes of the outside of his building and then the inside of his apartment. It was there that I met LeRoy for the second time.

It was a sunny Wednesday morning. LeRoy was CHCS's only full-time client able to live on his own. He lived in an assisted-living apartment complex very close to downtown on 6th Street. The only assistance LeRoy received here was one meal a day from a live-in volunteer for a Meals-on-Wheels–type service. He was never very friendly, at least to me, but I could probably chalk that up to not knowing why some sneaky college student was always hanging out with a fifty-year-old disabled guy.

LeRoy was surrounded by elderly acquaintances twenty years his senior. The first time I walked into the building, though, I screwed up a bit and set the tone for the next year as far as the people feeling comfortable around me. I could not find the correct key to get through the front door and into the lobby. I fumbled for what felt like an hour, going through the same set of keys over and over, looking like some nefarious hoodlum coming to steal their medicine money, threatening them through glass while they sat on that older-folk floral couch or leaned up against their locked-in-place walkers or were just too blind to see me whatsoever.

After what was more realistically a timespan of three or four minutes, Scottie—a Scottish immigrant with a war-mangled right hand—opened the door and asked me if I needed help, if I were lost, and who I was looking for. Scottie had a thick accent, one I was jealous of, and he greeted me that morning and every day thereafter with a shaky, "Hello, son." He was the only one who did not seem put off by my presence.

I told Scottie why I was there and who I needed to see, and he obliged by taking me by the hand with

LEROY

absolutely no hesitation and leading me to the elevators. I pressed the big round white "4" button that lit up a faded yellow. I was definitely going to the fourth floor to meet LeRoy in his own apartment now. No more neutral turf.

LeRoy's apartment was the last one on the left at the end of a long hallway. Completely unsure of what to expect, I leaned in gently and pressed my ear up against the cold steel door, listening for any life on the other side. I heard the garbled sounds of a television show. I took a deep breath and knocked loudly on the door. Nothing.

I waited a full minute or so and knocked again, louder than before. After about a second, I heard the scraping of metal on linoleum, a pause, and a barely audible moan. Another second later, I heard the heavy stomp of a foot followed by a soft dragging sound. The door ripped open so fast, it startled me, and I took a big step back. The door was stopped by the firm tug of a steel-chain bolt. I looked through the crack between the door and its frame, and I was met with the spectacle-covered left eye of a bearded face.

"Yeah?" LeRoy said through pursed lips, opening them just enough to speak but not enough to let the grit between his lips fall out.

"Hey, LeRoy. It's me, Dan. We're supposed to work together today."

LeRoy did not respond to me verbally. He looked

me in the eye and followed my body down to my boots.

Realizing LeRoy had no idea who I was, I tried to jog his memory a bit. "We met a couple days ago at the house on 22nd Street. You hurt your hand."

The bearded face with the glasses disappeared altogether, and the door closed. I just stood there with no idea what to do. I figured he was not going to let me in—that is, until I heard the familiar sound of a chain lock sliding out of its groove, dropping, swinging out from the door, and snapping back into the holder. The door opened, but only a bit. Through the crack he was making me become so familiar with, I watched as LeRoy limped back to his kitchen table. I stepped over the threshold cautiously, hoping these odd actions were the makeup of an unorthodox invitation. I mean, even if I were a vampire, I don't think this would have sufficed as an open invitation.

LeRoy neared the kitchen table, which was covered in papers and foodstuff. He put his cigarette down in the glass grooves of his ashtray, stepped completely in front of his metal kitchen chair, steadied himself for a moment, then stumbled backwards hard into his seat like an falling oak. The television was on and the volume fluctuated every one or two minutes as LeRoy constantly raised and lowered Matt Dillon's voice on a TV Land rerun of *Gunsmoke*. I stood in the kitchen area, still unsure about what I was supposed be doing. I was worried about offending him, but I didn't even know what would or would not do so.

"Hey, LeRoy, did you know this was the longest-running television drama in the history of television?" I asked, desperately wanting to break the silence. That silence was an awkwardness that over time would become comfortable, encouraged, and quite welcomed. But this first day, it was unbearable and making me anxious.

Without looking at this new kid invading his apartment, LeRoy said, "Yeah." Perhaps he did in fact know this trivia I spouted. But then he lowered the TV volume by half, and I realized LeRoy likely hadn't even heard me ask the pointless trivia question.

LeRoy took a drag off his cigarette. "What do we got to mow today?"

This was great! Right, of course—work. We could talk about work. We had to go to work together. This filled me with an excited surge of energy, and with the assistance of that badly needed adrenaline, I remembered the name of the guy JB told me to contact. The guy was supposed to tell me what lawns LeRoy needed to mow and if any other work needed to be done. This was a guy LeRoy knew: Rob Something.

"I think we're supposed to call Rob. Do you know Rob?" I asked the man focused on the three cowboys accosting Miss Kitty. LeRoy stood up with difficulty; it looked as if it hurt to get up and down in any general way. LeRoy disappeared down a very short hallway and into what looked like a bathroom. None of the lights were on in the whole apartment, which made it hard to see anything beyond where I was standing.

Once he was out of sight, I surveyed the apartment. I don't know why, but my first instinct was to open the fridge. I think you can tell a lot about people by what they keep in their refrigerators. I nervously looked back to what I assumed was the bathroom. I heard LeRoy moving around in there through the closed door. Spooked, I quickly went to the fridge and opened it up. The first thing that struck me as odd was that it was packed with a dozen white paper bags. There were also dozens of packages of condiments and single-serve silverware, three huge jars of mayo, a coffee tin, and half a chicken that had been in there a while.

I looked back toward the bathroom again. I didn't want LeRoy to catch me snooping around his place—figured it would make a shitty first impression. I closed the fridge and shifted my attention to the kitchen table, which was covered with opened and unopened mail, including several months of *Playboy* magazines still in their packaging. There were wires covering the table—I couldn't make out what they were. I also saw four unwound wire hangers, and next to these was a small wicker basket full of batteries. There was another wicker basket full of lighters, plus even more lighters scattered about. Five packs of cigarettes were open, and a sixth was still in its cellophane.

LEROY

I moved into the living room. The blue couch with a few cigarette burns had seen better days. I peered back at the bathroom one more time. The door was still closed. On top of the TV stand were three picture frames with photos of strangers. They most likely came with the frames. They did not look like real people LeRoy would know. The photos looked professionally taken and staged in that tacky sort of way sample photos have a tendency to be. On the shelves below the TV were knickknacks from a dollar store: a mermaid sitting on a rock, a wooden cat, two snow globes with Christmas scenes, and wicker baskets with receipts and more batteries. There was a random picture of LeRoy when he was younger (not a child, but not forty) and a small wooden bowling pin on the bottom shelf.

The room had a window air conditioning unit but also three huge standing fans—none of which were on. Next to the worn couch was an end table with yet another wicker basket filled with mail, receipts, batteries, and lighters. The walls were stained yellow, and a couple unframed, generic starving artist "paintings" decorated them.

The bathroom door opened as soon as I set foot back into the kitchen. LeRoy walked down the hall toward the kitchen and stopped at the huge white phone mounted on the wall with oversized numbers. A sheet of paper was tacked to the wall above the phone, listing names and phone numbers in big black letters.

The first name at the top was "ROB," followed by his number. LeRoy read the number to himself and dialed it. The phone cord was the longest I have ever seen. It trailed behind him like a curly umbilical cord as he walked back to his chair and crashed down as he had the time before. LeRoy waited for a moment until someone spoke on the other end.

"What are we mowin' today?" LeRoy asked Rob. I could hear mumbling on the other end. "Yeah . . . he's here," LeRoy said. He handed me the phone. "It's for you."

I grabbed the horn, and LeRoy slid back to his favorite position: facing the television with his ashtray at a thirty-degree angle to his left.

"Hello, Rob?"

"Yeah, who is this?" he asked. He had a deep, sheepish, and calming voice.

"Dan—Dan Monroe."

There was a pause filled with a long utterance of "*Uh* . . ." It was apparent Rob was doing something at that moment that demanded his attention more than the conversation I was attempting to have with him.

When he finished whatever it was he was doing, Rob went on to tell me the details of the day. He informed me he was going to be at the Circle Drive house. We were to meet him there, and he'd give us the list of all the houses LeRoy would mow that day. Some of the houses needed more work than just mowing, and he would give us another list with those houses too. He said LeRoy would mostly know all about that stuff.

From the background, LeRoy yelled out, "Rob!" raising his torso just slightly out of his chair.

Rob chuckled a bit over the phone. "Tell Buchholz he better be ready to work today."

I thanked him and hung up. Right off the bat, I could not tell if this Rob guy was a jerk or what. But I shook it off and tried to get LeRoy's attention. "Hey, LeRoy." His gaze didn't break from *Gunsmoke*. I just assumed he was listening and continued, "Rob said we gotta head over to a place called Circle Drive."

LeRoy turned down the volume, looked over at me, and held up his cigarette, which I immediately interpreted as, "Not until I'm done with this." LeRoy turned the volume back up and turned back to Matt Dillon, who was rescuing a Jewish prairie boy put into a coma by some no-good cowboy bandits. He smoked his cigarette, finished his coffee, and lit another cigarette before turning off the TV.

LeRoy stood up with difficulty, and without excusing himself, walked past me, nearly through me, and past the kitchen. He limped into the bathroom again. I stood for a few minutes getting uncomfortable, listening to LeRoy pee. I turned the television back on and watched the last few minutes of *Gunsmoke*, not knowing exactly what was going on with the coma-bound Jewish boy and the bandits, having missed the previous ten minutes.

The toilet flushed and the door opened, but no LeRoy emerged. There was the sound of something akin to a spray bottle being worked overtime. I leaned back on the recliner, attempting to peek through the hallway to see what LeRoy was doing. I saw in the reflection of the indigent, apartment-issued mirror that LeRoy was spraying himself—his entire upper body still in his tank top—with some sort of something.

LeRoy appeared from the bathroom and was shimmering. He looked as if he just got out of a very disturbing hot tropics lineup. I could smell the coconut right away and figured out that the man now standing in the kitchen with me had lathered himself up with tanning lotion—a shit-ton of tanning lotion. LeRoy was already browner than brown. His arms looked like that of Magda, the neighbor lady from *There's Something about Mary*.

He stood there glistening and slippery as he filled a gigantic thermos with coffee from an even larger pot of piping hot Folgers. It looked like a dangerous transfer of liquids, but no burning of hands took place; this transfer was completed gracefully. No matter how hot it got during the Wisconsin summer, LeRoy would always drink his hot coffee. It was like Chileans eating hot peppers straight-up out in the South American heat in order to stay cool. It seemed to be some sort of battle—fighting fire with fire. It was nearly impossible for me to draw any logical conclusions from LeRoy's habits, and it was fascinating.

LeRoy walked around the apartment looking once, twice, three times to make sure all his cigarette butts were out, his appliances and electronic devices were shut off, and nothing was out of sorts. I waited for him with the front door wide open, leaning up against it with a posture that attempted to make LeRoy aware I was not trying to rush him. LeRoy responded with a glare that still made me seem impatient as he walked out the door, right past me. Without looking in my direction at all, he barked, "Last one out locks the door."

I reached in and locked the door handle from the inside as I began to pull it shut. I didn't worry about locking up because of that enormous, cumbersome keychain with what had to have been over a dozen keys. Many had long lost their doors and locks, but I felt assured his apartment key was on there somewhere.

"*Wait!*" LeRoy suddenly yelped. He was out of eye shot, all the way down the hall, but I could hear him hustling back to the door, his keys jangling to the rhythm of a sluggish gate. LeRoy dramatically thrust himself between me, the door, and the frame. He rushed in and disappeared from my sight.

"What's up, LeRoy? You okay?" I asked to nothing, to wherever he was.

LeRoy came back into view from his hallway and

held up a brown bottle of spray-on tanning lotion. He held it high over his head. "Don't worry—I got it. Can't go out without this."

"You really need that?"

LeRoy stopped dead in his tracks about five inches from my face. "Yep."

On our second attempt to leave, we walked slowly down the long hallway that smelled too much of a nursing home for my taste. A loud *ding* announced the elevator was on its way up. This particular elevator moved at the pace of most of the residents, but we couldn't take the stairs on account of LeRoy's limp. Most stairs were a bitch for him, although he would never say so.

The noise of the elevator acted as a Pavlovian tuning fork. It startled LeRoy and shook a nervous thought out his mouth. "Did I put my cigarette out?" He motioned back toward the hallway that lead to his apartment.

I went to grab his arm. That is, I did not actually grab it, but I motioned that way. "Yeah, you put it out, buddy."

I was not 100 percent sure he had put it out, but I was pretty sure, and I didn't want him to be late for his first job with me in charge. LeRoy turned around, and I held the elevator as he limped in like a bruised boxer, carrying himself with enough pride to make me insecure.

LEROY

Down the elevator, past Scottie and half a dozen other staring eyes, and out the front door, we crossed the street to where the Jeep sat. When we got in the car, I realized I had no idea where this Circle Drive house was. I assumed LeRoy knew nothing about it—something I would assume with so many other things. But LeRoy told me where it was right away. He could not tell me streets or anything, but he could explain what it was near and what to drive by. "Turn here, go there" kind of stuff. Like an untrusting dick, I instead called Rob and got directions from him. I didn't know yet to trust LeRoy's unique gift of spatial recall—though I would later on.

As it turned out, LeRoy was pretty dead-on. When we pulled into the driveway, he shouted out, "See! See! I know where to go."

He went on and on, telling me that I should have believed him, that he knew where the house was, that no one ever listens to him, and that I was no different. Great fucking start, hey? LeRoy was right—he did know what he was talking about—but I gave him an unintentionally embarrassed and slightly dirty look anyway. LeRoy smiled while making sure not to look at me. He rarely looked at me or most people, for that matter.

LeRoy opened the Jeep door and lit a cigarette immediately with his ass still on the seat, one leg out the door. Like a fat garden slug, he left a trail of tanning lotion down the seat and on the door. He closed the door hard, really hard. Once he took his first drag, he stopped, turned around, went back to the Jeep, opened it up, and pulled out the huge coffee thermos. He drug his leg as he walked up over the curb and sat down on a stump by the garage.

A very tall man I assumed was Rob came out from the back of the house, his frame moving gracefully and quickly to LeRoy. I jogged to catch up. The two of us shook hands while reintroducing ourselves. I would come to very quickly realize Rob really was fantastic, a great guy—not the smartass-slave-driver persona I had so quickly slapped on him back at LeRoy's apartment. Rob was about nine feet tall, and he was wearing paint-and-grease-stained khaki shorts and an XL or XXL T-shirt that hung off his skinny frame as if he were a hanger. He had a nice haircut; it didn't look cheap, although it most likely was. His shirt shared the same colors as the shorts, slapped with some sort of paint-and-maintenance-related stains. He walked with huge strides and a clipboard with a list fastened to it.

Without missing a stride, he turned his head and looked at LeRoy. "You're on the clock, Buchholz. We don't pay you to drink coffee."

Thinking again maybe this Rob character was actually an asshole, I watched LeRoy. I hawked in on LeRoy's face, and there was nothing but an ear-to-ear grin. I focused my attention back on Rob, who happened to be wearing the exact same smile. Rob was in fact not an asshole. Rob would never do one thing in the next two years to even remotely resemble an asshole.

"Hey, Buchholz. Buchholz!" he called out. LeRoy shot him a glare. "The lawn mower is filled up, so start whenever you're ready."

LeRoy stood up and took a step toward Rob. "This is client abuse," LeRoy barked back at Rob. "I'm telling JB." With a smile, LeRoy paused for a moment and thrust his neck out a bit farther, waiting for a response from Rob. When he did not get one, he waved him off with a limp-wristed "Bah!"

There was never any babying of LeRoy whenever Rob was around. Yet Rob never harped on him or hounded him. He did not tell him smoking was bad, as did so many others. (As if LeRoy hadn't a clue that what he was doing was detrimental to his health.) Rob never hovered over LeRoy to make sure he was doing things right. Rob knew LeRoy knew what he was doing and let him do his work uninterrupted.

LeRoy turned around, squatted back down next to the garage, and took a drag of his cigarette far away from the gas canister, which was by the edge of the driveway. He put his head down. As Rob started to speak again, LeRoy lifted his right hand, the hand with the cigarette in it, letting Rob know he'd get to work when he was finished with the Winston that smoldered at his fingertips. Rob saw LeRoy's gesture, and familiar with it as he was, he nodded with a playful, almost brotherly smirk and waved off whatever he was going to say.

I ran up to Rob, not really knowing what I was supposed to be doing. Rob, sensing my movement, stopped in his tracks and turned around to face me. He patted me on the shoulder two times and left his hand on me like a long-fingered bear paw while we walked across the lawn.

"All right, let's get you that list."

Rob and I sat on two makeshift stools near the front of the garage, below snow shovels and rakes. There were two big tricycles in the garage. Both were blue and looked as if they hadn't been used in quite some time. As Rob wrote the list of all the lawns LeRoy has to mow and directions to each one, he hummed to himself. It sounded like "Sympathy for the Devil."

"Stones?" I asked.

Rob stopped writing, looked at me from the corner of his eye, and smiled. "Yeah," he said, nodding his head in approval. "I love the Stones. You like them?"

"I love the Stones, man."

"Good."

Rob handed me the scribbled list. The writing was barely legible—blue scratchy lines covered the page—but I was too shy to ask him what each one said. I had no idea how, but I figured I would get the addresses from someone else. Rob slapped the notepad methodically against his thigh, looked up, and pursed his lips, thinking. He sighed.

"You and LeRoy are gonna have to do some pressing maintenance work and landscaping here and there throughout most of the summer," he said.

I liked the sound of that. I had worked as a garbage man and on a farm for some time. I liked manual labor. I excitedly told Rob, "Yeah, of course, man. Whatever you need."

I was getting the sense I was going to love this job. I was already having such a good time. And it wasn't an "I'm doing something good!" false-sense-of-superiority-bull-shitty feeling, which is what it usually feels like.

Rob was talking when the stentorian rumble of a starting lawn mower interrupted our discussion. Rob patiently waited for the distraction to subside, then informed me every house, with the exception of two, had its own lawn mower. It was the good kind too, the kind that doesn't have a starter cord. All you had to do was prime it a couple times, hold the starter button, squeeze the handles together, and start it right up. LeRoy and I would have to transport one of these mowers to the two exception homes.

"Can you transport a mower in your Jeep?" Rob asked. "I'm just asking because sometimes people don't like putting mowers in their vehicles—it gets grassy and oily and stuff."

"No, that's fine," I said. "I don't care. I mean,

that's what Jeeps are for, right?"

Rob and I were unable to carry on our conversation any longer with the lawn mower screaming over us. Rob put up his long, E.T. index finger, giving me the universal signal for "hold on a minute." As LeRoy got farther and farther down the long rectangular yard of the Circle Drive house, the sound faded to a low humming. We had only a few moments to put together a plan before the lawn shark looped its way back, drowning out our words once again.

Quickly as he could, Rob laid out a blueprint for the summer projects the three of us would attempt to finish in a fairly short period of time. Rob had a few projects already set up but told me there would be plenty more throughout the next three months. It seemed like a lot of work, and knowing nothing about anything, I innocently assumed it would be totally doable. Piece of cake. I was excited to know it would just be me, Rob, and LeRoy: an average college nobody, a seven-foot-tall Rolling Stones fanatic, and a fifty-year-old cognitively disabled, idiosyncratic sun worshiper.

It was not too long before we were interrupted yet again as LeRoy came around the side of the garage, limping along but cutting nothing but perfect, straight, even lines in the yard. Cutting himself off midword, Rob leaned back on the big plastic overturned paint barrel acting as his stool, knowing he could not compete with the sound of the mower LeRoy pushed past us.

LEROY

LeRoy, limping at an incredible speed for his impeding leg, looked at the two of us sitting by the garage and gave a half wave. Realizing we might not have seen the wave or understood what he was doing, he planted out two more fast waves. In doing so, he lost his balance and veered off his perfectly linear path. He pulled his waving hand down quickly, back to the handle, and focused every ounce of energy and concentration on the lawn. LeRoy was an artist; the mower, a large, noisy brush he stroked effortlessly over the canvas of the lawn. LeRoy had complete control over his work. Three times a week, he owned those lawns—they were his.

The days I worked with Rob were merely extensions of my philosophy classes: Philosophy of Maintenance 101 and Philosophy of LeRoy's Cognitive Mind 210. Rob taught me the quick-and-easy way of many tasks: building and staining decks; all facets of plumbing; remodeling bathrooms; framing and planking doors; ripping up and laying new carpet; grouting tile; rebuilding lawn mower motors; and removing blood, vomit, shit, piss, and coffee from carpets. He showed me how to hang cabinets (a massive pain in the ass, as were doors); plane countertops; set closets; and put in stoves, refrigerators, water heaters, and air conditioners. Rob and I took out and put in windows, put in stairs (another pain in the ass), and laid concrete. He picked up where Shelden left off, teaching me through example.

He reminded me how to be completely natural by actually being completely natural.

I clicked stop on the recorder and checked the battery. I started it back up with one battery bar left. Good thing I was rolling into town soon—I would definitely be needing batteries.

I took a look across the horizon. It was starting to snow, light at first but thickening up exponentially. Within seconds, through the dusting of white, I saw a green exit marker for Black River Falls, which immediately reminded me of my greatest and most memorable adventures with Rob and LeRoy.

Rob started working at CHCS when he was about my age, and he was now in his early thirties and working as CHCS's only maintenance man. He handled the work for the entire river valley region—literally all of it. I couldn't help but think Rob had to be somewhat relieved when I showed up, if for no other reason than it meant he didn't have to do every goddamn thing himself.

I worked with Rob consistently for about a year—a little more, maybe a little less. With an extra set of hands, Rob was able to get a lot more done. Before I showed up, Rob had all the same responsibilities, but he had only LeRoy to help him. It was not a burdensome task per se. But it put Rob in the position of constantly finding things for LeRoy to do. And as efficient as LeRoy was, he would finish the tasks quickly and was always looking for something new to do, pestering Rob for additional tasks. Most of the huge jobs LeRoy could not really help with either because he did not have enough balance and depth perception or because the jobs were just too dangerous. I find it necessary to mention that LeRoy didn't think they were too dangerous, even if they were, and Rob would never put him in any treacherous position. On top of that, after all their work, Rob would help LeRoy with LeRoy things: going to the doctor, getting socks, getting food, getting cigarettes, getting tickets for bowling, and more. So when I showed up, I definitely lightened the load for Rob, and I like to think he appreciated the break.

But it was a double-edged sword of sorts, as my help only opened Rob up to an even heavier workload.

LEROY

It was insane really, all the things Rob did. It was hard to comprehend how he got it all done before I showed up. Not that I was this great attribute or anything. It was just the sheer magnitude of his duties. It was daunting, at times seemingly impossible, even when the two of us worked together, let alone when he did it all on his own. No matter where the two or three of us went, whether it was one of the dozen houses or the main office, there was always someone bitching to Rob about something that needed to be done:

"Rob, the air conditioner needs to be replaced at Losey."

"Rob, there's a broken window at Circle Drive."

"Rob, make sure you get LeRoy over to 26th—it needs to be mowed."

"Rob, when are you going to get those doors hung at 16th?"

"Rob, the bathroom needs to be torn out and replaced at Black River."

"Rob, Judy needs her bed moved; where it is now makes her paranoid, and she can't sleep."

"Rob, a tree needs to be felled on Main."

"Rob, the rider lawn mower needs to be fixed, and it has a flat tire."

"Rob, Steve broke a fish tank, and it needs to be cleaned up."

"Rob, Sam punched a hole in the wall."

"Rob, hook up new phones on 22nd Street."

"Rob, trim the bushes."

"Rob, build a sandbox."

"Rob, hang a tire swing on 7th."

"Rob, the porch on State needs a wheelchair ramp."

"Rob, when are you going to install that air conditioner at Losey?"

What blew my mind above all else was how damn impatient all of them were. Rob was one guy, and the never-ending list of shit he had to do was quite literally never-ending. Most of the jobs were taxing and in a normal world would have been handled by a contractor and a team. Not that Rob wasn't qualified; he most certainly was. Rob was a contractor of sorts—an underappreciated, gently pissed on, quiet contractor. It was a difficult spot to be in, but Rob always took his to-do list, clasped it to the beat-up wooden clipboard he compulsively carried with him, smiled under a hushed sigh, got his lanky ass in the truck, and went on to the next job.

Once I became comfortable with Rob, I asked him about all the shit he had to do and how he felt about his thankless duties. We were getting in the truck, heading to one job or another.

"Jesus, man—they're relentless, aren't they?" I said.

Rob just looked at me and smiled. He turned the key. The whole cab shook with discomfort, as if telling the driver this was the absolute last time it would start up. Without a word, he jammed a cassette converter into his tape deck, connecting it to a portable CD player. He blew dust from a Rolling Stones greatest hits CD, snapped it into the old scratched-up player, and pressed play.

"You like the Stones, right?" he asked.

"Yeah, of course," I replied.

Rob, having clearly heard my question about the relentless work, was ignoring it. That was it. Rob never bitched, never complained, and never badmouthed anyone. I wished I were like that. I was not.

Rob and I always listened to quality music when we tooled around La Crosse. The playlist included the Stones, Led Zeppelin, the Doors, A Perfect Circle, Tool, and a little Nine Inch Nails. We listened to Radiohead and the Pixies in the morning, and in the hot summer afternoons, we jammed out to the Cars and the Talking Heads.

Every once in a while, the three of us would have to head two hours northeast to work on one house CHCS had in the small town of Black River Falls. All three of us packed into Rob's red beater—Rob behind the wheel, LeRoy in shotgun, and me always riding bitch—while the Rolling Stones blared in front of us through the muffled speakers like a purposeful voice discouraging us from partaking in any meaningless banter we may have felt inclined to strike up.

We followed the set routine when it came to

getting into Rob's truck: LeRoy opened the passenger door in a polite *after you* manner. I cordially nodded and in an overly hurried manner hoisted myself up into the truck and slid my ass across the worn gray cloth seat into the middle position. As I sat in the middle alone in the truck, LeRoy lit up a grit and leaned on the open passenger door, stressing the hinges to their maximum strength. Rob then stepped up and lowered his seven-foot frame into the truck, ducking his head in such an overzealous way that can only be explained by an infinite number of prior hits of the head on the door's frame.

Rob looked over at LeRoy. "Hey, Lah-Roy, let's get the show on the road." ("Lah-Roy" being an overdrawn nickname Rob often used for him.)

Taking another drag, LeRoy indicated to Rob he'd be in a minute.

Rob never let LeRoy smoke in his truck due to the aforementioned CHCS policy. Rob knew I let LeRoy smoke in my Jeep, and I doubt he gave a shit I did so. Rob didn't smoke, so I'm sure it was easier for him to follow the rule than it was for me.

Rob asked me, "So you know why LeRoy has to sit shotgun, I see."

"Actually, no, I don't." I said. I just assumed LeRoy liked the window for some weird LeRoy reason.

"Well, have you noticed how LeRoy locks the door every time he gets settled in his seat?"

LEROY

I thought for a minute, and I did in fact recall that every time LeRoy got in the truck or even the Jeep, he locked the door immediately and would roll the window down. He'd grab the door with both arms as if he were attempting to carry it, then he'd give it a good hard shake. My interest piqued.

"Yeah, what's up with that?"

Rob grinned. "I'll tell ya sometime."

LeRoy sucked his grit down past the recession of the filter, put the butt out in the palm of his hand, and put it in the front left pocket of his pants, as he had done a hundred times before and would do hundred times after. At the time, it was still such an odd habit to me, regardless of his repetition, and it made me uneasy. I looked at Rob, and he sensed my uneasiness.

"Can you believe that? Crazy ol' Buchholz. Buchholz, you're crazy!"

LeRoy patted his pocket, making sure the ash was good and dead, pulled his sagging pants up around his emaciated hips, and stretched the truck door farther open than it was supposed to go. As he got into the truck, he slid hard into my right side, almost hurting me, and he slammed the door so incredibly hard, it hurt our ears.

"Jesus, Buchholz. Easy," Rob scolded.

LeRoy always slammed the door that hard. He looked at the door intensely, inspecting the location of the lock. LeRoy locked the door and threw his body against it as if he were testing its durability. He slammed into it hard a second time, like a ram attacking a potential threat.

As uneasy as his actions could make me at times, I could watch LeRoy partake in his idiosyncratic rituals for hours. There were times I felt as if I were just there to observe the man, just to watch, just to be amazed and to take notes, as if I would later be called on to recount his actions. Most of the time, I felt as though I were simply there to prevent anything horrible from happening to him and, if the opportunity arose, to protect him. And although this was a superficial badge of honor I had pinned on myself, it felt wonderful and important.

Rob, staring straight ahead, revealed another sly grin. "Hey, Lah-Roy, remember when you fell out of the truck?"

Before I could even think the words *holy* and *shit*, LeRoy spoke: "Yeah," he said, matching Rob's grin but all the while shaking his head from side to side in a disapproving manner. For a moment, I thought they were having a goof at my expense. But soon enough, LeRoy's grin morphed into an angry face, as if *we* were having a goof on *him*. He got a little pissy.

Rob leaned over and started telling me the story quietly. He whispered, even though he really didn't seem to care if LeRoy could hear him. LeRoy continued to shake his head, as if doing so would stop the story from being told.

"We were going about twenty-five miles an hour on 1st Street, and the door popped right open. You know how hard Lah-Roy leans on that bastard, right? So, sure enough, he went right out, right through the door."

I could not believe what I was hearing.

"I swerved like crazy, and I reached out just in time, caught him by his belt, and yanked him back into the truck. We were both pretty shook up, weren't we, Lah-Roy?"

LeRoy ignored Rob's question—not really embarrassed, just annoyed Rob was telling the story.

"I think I even busted a couple of your belt loops when I yanked ya back in, didn't I?" he asked LeRoy, who still chose to ignore him.

I chuckled in disbelief and mentally added this story to my unending cache of crazy shit LeRoy had been involved in.

"Right, Lah-Roy?" Rob egged on

By now, the three of us were on Highway 16, drifting toward northeastern Wisconsin. Minute after minute went by, and it was quiet until Rob broke the silence. "Maybe it wouldn't have happened if someone had been wearing his seatbelt."

LeRoy kept his stare out the window steadfast and pushed Rob's words away with a waving hand, as if he were brushing crumbs out of the air in front of him.

"But that ain't gonna happen, is it, Buchholz?" Rob asked no one in particular.

After a moment of contempt, LeRoy finally chuckled and shook his head not so maniacally, but noticeably, all the while smiling a big-ass, LeRoy smile.

They were quite infrequent, but I always looked forward to our long trips out to Black River Falls. It was a beautiful drive. If you've never been out that way, I recommend it; the Wisconsin woods set against the backdrop of the river valley bluffs can make time stop. I only made it up there three times at the most. Because it was a special trip, we would take the opportunity to burn a new CD, usually some up-and-down classic compilation. Rob's truck did not have air conditioning, so we cranked the windows all the way down and let the sweet smell of freshly mowed grass, manure-reeking cow fields, endless soybean farms, and the Wisconsin corn stalks overwhelm our nostrils as we sat content, never talking very much at all. On occasion, LeRoy would see something he had never seen before, or something he had seen but had simply forgotten, and he would elbow me in my rib cage and point to it. I would nod monotonously and tell him what it was, if he asked. LeRoy would nod in return.

On one particular morning drive up to Black River Falls, we were on a stretch flanked by soybean fields. We were cruising shakily at sixty miles per hour when a large mass of blackbirds exploded into the sky, spooked by something unknown to us. As they rose up in front of us in the distance, they became even with the horizon, then, in a fluid movement almost undetectable to us, they double back toward the truck. The birds' eclipse blotted out completely the sun that only seconds ago had been making the three of us uncomfortably hot. And like that, they were gone altogether.

LeRoy whipped back and stared through the roof of the truck as if he could see them flying overhead. As he sat turned around almost completely, watching them head back south, he said, smiling and nodding in agreement with himself, "They're going back to La Crosse."

He paused and turned back around, facing Rob and me. "Hey, Dan. Hey, Rob. Hey." LeRoy looked at the both of us as he settled back into his seat. "You know those birds?" he asked.

Rob, not breaking his gaze from the road, answered, "Yeah, Buchholz, what about 'em?"

Satisfied someone had answered him, LeRoy went on, "Birds . . . those birds—birds must be tired all the time."

Both Rob and I ignored LeRoy's comment and brushed him off with a generic "Sure."

Now dissatisfied with our lack of continuing engagement, LeRoy went back to facing forward. He sat quietly for a minute. "Wonder when they sleep," he said to himself.

In the quiet that followed, I actually thought about LeRoy's seemingly innocuous statements. I was suddenly overcome with a feeling of comfort. I smiled as it dawned on me that, yes, birds must be tired a lot from all the flying. I mean, when was the last time you stumbled upon a sleeping bird?

"That's a good point, LeRoy," I replied ten or so minutes after he initially presented his statement to us.

"I didn't say anything," LeRoy spat out.

I let it go, but I thought it a good lesson about not brushing him off anymore—something I had previously told myself I would no longer do, yet there I was, still doing it. LeRoy was someone to be paid attention to. Whether he was making a comment about birds or asking Rob if he could smoke, knowing the answer to always be no, this was how we passed the time.

We drove, drank Mountain Dew and endless to-go cups of coffee, laughed, and enjoyed each other's company—all in the name of life. Every twenty minutes or so, LeRoy would bring up what appeared to be some asinine topic. But once I thought about it a few hours later, it would reveal itself as some pertinent philosophical tidbit or a brilliant and logical observation we had never thought over before. This way of passing the time and understanding the importance of LeRoy's words would go on for 118 miles, and I longed for 118 more.

By the time we reached Black River Falls, we were hot, ornery, and cramped—all three of us squeezed into that sardine-can cab and all three of us not that small at all. After numerous trips to Home Depot, Farm & Fleet, and Menards, we finally had an acceptable, but not impressive, arsenal to attack the bathroom project the powers that be had handed down to Rob.

I knew CHCS did the best they could with what they had, and with that truthfully being said, they did a damn good job. However, these houses take a beating with the particular tenants who inhabit them. Some of these particular tenants are a little rougher and more unforgiving on their surroundings than the average house tenant: smashing, knocking, spilling, punching, kicking, falling, throwing, spinning, spitting, loving, and hating. Because Rob—or LeRoy and I, for that matter—could not make it out to Black River Falls as often as we would have liked, the house suffered from neglect a bit more than the others. It was not neglected in an unlivable manner—not at all. It just received less upkeep due to geographical restrictions and impossibilities. Rob got up to that house only once a month, if not every three.

In the case of this particular project, the main-level bathroom floor was rotting out in a creeping fashion, and the bathtub and shower unit needed to be replaced. Basically, the entire room, except for the sink, was to be gutted and replaced in less than two days. Not a small task for a twenty-one-year-old nonlicensed "construction worker," a foreman who was running all over the place fixing everything else in the goddamn house, and his cognitively depressed sidekick.

Tearing up the floor was not too bad, considering half of it was so soft, it felt wet and held on to our hands with its tacky fingerlings as we lifted it. With the first two layers of floor gone, we could see through the piping and straight down beneath us into the basement.

I asked Rob, "Is this safe any way whatsoever? Are we going to crash through to the basement to our deaths?"

Rob stopped his work, looked through the floor, put pressure on a couple random areas, and tapped a couple pipes with the steel toe of his boots. "Step here, here, and here. Not there or there . . . or there," he informed me, pointing.

"Are you shitting me?" As he resumed his work, I took the answer to be no.

As you all know by now, LeRoy's balance was shit. He could not move around easily or fluidly—any dreams of being a dancer had long been dashed. His balance was even worse when he found himself in cramped places, such as the bathroom. Because of this, Rob gave LeRoy a bunch of random tasks he knew LeRoy could handle elsewhere. In reality, LeRoy could handle pretty much any task by himself. Rob never needed to bother him much at all or worry when he was off far away working on something else.

LeRoy's task this day was a lock in the basement

that needed to be replaced. Rob had initially asked me to take care of the door and its defiant lock. For over an hour, I tried, I really tried, to get that piece of shit lock off. The screws had been stripped completely, thus making it impossible to remove. I attempted to execute what Rob had taught me about removing stripped screws. Apparently, the trick is to use a screw driver one size bigger than the screws' original grooves. If you use a bigger screw driver, it will, in theory, connect with the slight remnants of the original grooves. And if you are sweet enough to it and move slowly enough, it will pull the screw out. In theory. However, during my embarrassing attempt to extract these stripped screws, I made the situation much, much worse. Trying to help, I ruined the screws beyond any real form of repair.

Feeling defeated and silly, I walked halfway up the steeply ominous stairs, looking up at Rob through the missing floorboards and skinny pipes. "I can't get a hold on the screws," I admitted. "Yeah, I'm pretty sure I made it a helluva lot worse."

Not looking away from his work, Rob told me to give him a minute and he would take a look himself. Having expected him to be more pissed off and relieved he was not, I went back down into the basement and walked over to study the mess I had made of the situation.

After a few minutes, I heard Rob's size fourteen boots, which matched his epically tall frame, hurriedly coming down the steps, like a child tumbling down the stairs to his playroom. He squatted in front of the door handle and wrung his hands together like a maniacal villain who had just tied his victim to a railroad track. He tilted his head from side to side, like a bird looking into the open knot of a tree.

"Well, shit, that's shitty. We'll figure it out."

Rob never got mad. Look up *laid back* in the dictionary, and there will be a picture of Rob shrugging and drinking a Coke. Seriously, look it up.

"Where's Lah-Roy?" he asked me.

"Last I saw him . . ." I paused to think exactly where that was. "Oh! He was outside, by the side of the house, working by some shrubs."

"Shrubs?" he repeated.

"Yeah, he was dickin' around with a tree stump, it looked like."

Rob remembered instantaneously, as I did, that during the drive up, he had mentioned a stump that needed to be cut out because it was housing ants or some other clan of mischievous insects. Rob thought for a minute, lips pursed and hands on hips, and waved me along as he headed out the door.

We searched around the big Victorian house, playing Marco Polo, until we eventually came upon LeRoy, who did not see us approach from behind. At that particular second, LeRoy was holding an axe above his head, ready to assault the deadened remnants of an oak tree.

"Oh, shit," Rob yelped under his breath as his walk quickened to a run. "LeRoy! Put—the—axe—down."

LeRoy nearly jumped out of his khakis and dropped the axe behind his back.

"Jesus, LeRoy!" Rob shouted. "What are you doing with an axe?"

Startled and out of breath, LeRoy almost apologized. (*Almost* was as close to apologizing as LeRoy ever got.) "I'm just doing the work you told me to do. This is abuse, client abuse!" he said, pointing one finger high into the air, proclaiming an important note, demanding his exoneration. His voice got higher and higher, uncomfortably pitched, as he fake complained.

"You don't get to use an axe," Rob said. "Like, ever."

LeRoy limped over to Rob and me while dusting off his hands. "I'm telling JB. This is client abuse, straight and simple. Client abuse." He threatened us with a familiar grin that made us grin just because he was so goddamned amused with himself.

As LeRoy picked the axe up from the ground, Rob playfully and safely ripped it from his dirty, leathered hands. "Yeah, yeah, yeah. Always complaining, Buchholz."

Rob reached over and pulled LeRoy in just a bit as he put his arm around his shoulder—not pulling him in too close, not forcing him anywhere, just letting LeRoy move naturally and comfortably. Rob told LeRoy he had a job for him down in the basement.

LeRoy absolutely hated leaving work unfinished and almost never did, unless it was a huge project he understood would take longer than the usual time allotted. LeRoy looked back and forth between the shrubs he had been working with and the tree stump he had been abruptly prohibited from removing. He looked at Rob, then at the pile, then at the stump, then back at Rob—faster and faster and faster, now completely animated, turning his head so hard you'd have thought it'd fall off.

Rob shook his head back at LeRoy. "Don't worry about it. You can come back to it when you're done." He spoke in such a calm, matter-of-fact manner, it made LeRoy content enough for the time being.

We made our way down to the basement, glancing up to the bathroom above. Rob showed LeRoy the lock and the doorknob that needed to be removed. Rob gave LeRoy a vast array of screwdrivers to assail the lock, then looked to me. "C'mon, Dan."

Once again, Rob and I ascended the basement steps, went around the corner, and headed back to the bathroom from hell. Right before we went in, Rob stopped and turned back to me. He hunkered down, not squatting but attempting to get as close to eye level with me—his much, much shorter helper monkey—as possible. He raised his eyebrows. "Now, that should keep him busy for the afternoon." Rob laid out a mischievous smile, one that let me know he had given LeRoy an impossible task.

Rob and I looked down to where the bathroom floor used to be earlier that morning. Our task now was getting the bathtub out of the corner and putting in the new one. It was not until we looked at the chasm in front of us that we realized we most certainly should have removed the tub *first* and then the floor.

"Well, shit," Rob said.

Nothing we could do about it now. Getting the tub unadhered from its corner was not nearly as difficult or time consuming as we thought. We had it almost completely out when we heard the carnival rattling of key chains announcing the arrival of LeRoy Buchholz.

As he approached, I yelled out a common LeRoy request: "Smoke break?" I predicted.

Not hearing me or just ignoring me, two equally probable theories, LeRoy walked into the bathroom—completely unaware it was missing its floor. With one foot over nothing but air, LeRoy did one of those Wile E. Coyote things, where he was leaning over the open floor, grasping for the doorframe, barely keeping himself from falling into the abyss below. All physical comedy aside, he really did almost fall through it, and our hearts did skip a beat.

"There's no floor," LeRoy informed us.

Rob gave him a dirty look followed by the smile.

"There's no floor, Dan. Bathrooms need floors."

"Whaddya need, LeRoy?"

"All done," he said.

Rob looked up immediately and smacked my shoulder twice, forcing my attention on LeRoy. In LeRoy's left hand was the entire doorknob. He held it up in the air, raising it over his head, shaking it like an idol.

"I'm all done. Smoke break."

Rob looked at me, then back to LeRoy one more time. "Jesus, Buchholz."

LeRoy worked on that knob for no more than twenty minutes. I spent as much as an hour ripping and stripping that piece of shit knob beyond repair, and LeRoy geared up and got it out in twenty fucking minutes? What the hell?

LeRoy laughed through his nose and clenched teeth and asked Rob where he wanted him to put the mangled lock.

"In the bed of the truck, I guess," Rob told him.

"Where?" LeRoy asked again.

"Back of the truck, Buchholz. Throw it in the back of the truck. There's a new one in the bed. Install that one where the old one was. Dan can help you."

"I can do it," LeRoy argued. "I can do it. I don't need his help," LeRoy said smiling.

He walked out the door, and we could see the red truck behind him before he disappeared out of sight, then came right back into frame, whistling some no-name tune.

"Smoke break!"

It was really snowing now. The snow had gone from airy and blowing in the wind to wet and heavy in a short amount of time. It was as if the snow decided I hadn't been paying enough attention to it, and now it wanted me to notice. I stopped the recorder for a second so I could concentrate. I turned on my wipers, and checked the time.

I recognized the parallel military roads of Tomah, Wisconsin. I had driven past this area on more than one occasion with Antoine in the passenger seat. Even though the snow would slow me down some, I would be in La Crosse in less than an hour. I got excited for a moment, but that went away when I remembered what I was doing here. I pressed the red record button and thought about time.

One morning, we were sitting at his kitchen table, smoking cigarettes. LeRoy's roommate, Matt Dillon, joined us in the background, as he did most every morning. This particular day, he and Kitty the barmaid were dealing with the sexual tension they battled every episode.

I watched LeRoy as he took drag after drag of his grit. He wore thick, late-seventies-early-eighties-style spectacles. The lenses were large and held together by a prominent rim, which doubled its lines over the bridge of his nose. On each side, masking and Scotch tapes were wrapped tightly around the hinge screws, keeping everything intact more than was necessary. There were also tiny snail trails of some sort on the lenses that certainly had to obscure his view to some degree.

I asked, "Hey, what's all that shit on your glasses?"

"Superglue," he snapped.

"Why do you have superglue all over your glasses?"

"Keeps 'em together," he answered.

"LeRoy, my man, you need new glasses ASAP."

"I know I need new glasses. That's what I've been saying—I've needed new glasses forever."

"Forever?" I repeated, being a smartass. After working with him for so many months, I was comfortable enough to mess around with him, and he would dish it right back. "So you're telling me you've needed new glasses for the last forty-nine years?"

"That's what I'm tellin' ya."

Suddenly, LeRoy lost his balance and nearly jolted right off his seat, frantically trying to correct himself, as he looked around feverishly for something—I did not know what exactly. Whatever it was, he forgot about it almost as quickly as he had thought of it. LeRoy went right back to enjoying his cigarettes and coffee, two things he made sure are never depleted in stock.

I had a vision of LeRoy as Burgess Meredith in that episode of *The Twilight Zone*. Meredith has a shitty, nagging wife who gets rid of all his beloved books. After a nuclear fallout, he's the only one left on earth, and he now has an infinite supply of books. But instead of books, all LeRoy needed was an infinite supply of coffee and cigarettes—that was it.

He preferred his coffee and grits at the kitchen table surrounded by his remotes and tools, while Sassy sat next to him on his right—always on his right—on her own precious chair. LeRoy had his seat and Sassy had hers. I could always tell which was hers by the thick mat of hair blanketing it like suffocating gray ivy. Only that chair had a furry seat cover. However, Sassy was in fact a cat, and she wandered about, as cats do. One could only assume she had at least once or twice found her way onto his seat and he had subsequently lowered himself down into the chair. It may have explained LeRoy's bizarrely cautious behavior as he so fretfully avoided crushing her beneath him every morning.

LeRoy, cigarette in mouth, stood up now to check his seat. Seeing no sign of Sassy, he fell right back down with all his weight. But he forgot his coffee on the kitchen counter.

"Sonuvabitch!" he exclaimed.

It was very amusing when LeRoy had his rare cursing outbursts. He did not swear often, per se, or "cuss," as he called it. But sometimes he would just get so upset, and epic strings of profanities would billow out of his mouth like the smoke from his grits. This never made me uncomfortable—even the first time it happened. It was not as if he lost his head and went nuts or anything. It was comical and completely unthreatening. Most of the time, he barely used words at all. My favorite nonsensical curse word he barked out was *sucker bitch*. I really had to perk my ears the first few times he uttered it because he had strung the two words together so quickly.

The cussing really only came out when he got so frustrated with himself—when he forgot things, specifically. It seemed he felt genuinely disappointed in himself when his memory failed him, and it failed him often. I would attempt to calm these tirades LeRoy unleashed upon himself by telling him I forgot things all the time. But every time I said this, he just looked at me as if I were making it up just to make him feel better. Although I wasn't making it up in this particular case, most of the time he was pretty good at telling the difference.

But no matter how strongly LeRoy feigned belief that I forgot things too, whenever I did forget something, he would yell out, "Oh no! You forgot! I'm telling JB, and she's gonna find out and put you on hold for client abuse!" It was always, "You forgot my money," "You forgot my bank slips," or you-forgot-whatever. I would look LeRoy in the eye, lean in real close, and say, "You want client abuse? I'll show you client abuse," as I shook my fist at him until he smiled. He would give me that look, the look that said, *I know exactly what is going on*.

While LeRoy smoked his grits, drank his coffee, and watched *Gunsmoke* that morning, I called JB about getting him in to see his eye doctor. She gave me the number and a special code to use so the doctor's office could charge the appropriate offices.

This was when I figured out the whole time thing with LeRoy: He understood the concept of time, but he could not grasp it in clock terms. If he had an appointment at seven in the morning, he couldn't tell me that unless he read it off something. And if the appointment was at seven and I told him it was at three, he would not be able to correct me on that. So when he asked what time an appointment was, it would be much clearer if I said, "It's an hour and ten minutes from now."

For example, I told him his newly acquired optometry appointment was at ten. He looked at the clock in the kitchen, which he may or may not have known how to read, then asked me how much time he had until we had to leave. He was watching *Gunsmoke,* which started at nine. So I said, "We have to leave after *Gunsmoke.*" LeRoy's immediate reaction was to ask if he had enough time for a smoke. I told him he had time for more than one. He asked how long *Gunsmoke* was on, and I said it was on for one hour. We could watch most of it, and then we'd have to go.

Usually by that point, LeRoy got it. It wasn't nearly as tedious a process as it may seem. It really was the easiest way to instill a sense of time in him. It was all about relating time to pertinent information he was interested in. Pug also relayed time to LeRoy using this method. Keep in mind neither Pug nor I taught this method to the other. We just each figured out it was the best way to help LeRoy understand the concept of time.

LeRoy needed to be reminded about time, of course. But we all need to be reminded—or we all need to set reminders on our BlackBerries and our iPhones. We write Post-its to ourselves and put them on our fridges or our desks. I guess, quite simply, I was LeRoy's Post-it.

Gunsmoke had about fifteen minutes left when I told LeRoy he had to get ready to go. He sucked down his grit faster than I had ever seen anyone do so, hoisted himself up out of his chair, and headed into the bathroom. He came out a short time later, and we made it down to the Jeep and headed out to the hospital complex.

It was quiet in the car until we passed the frozen Black River and the waterway spurred a topic of conversation.

"Do you want to go ice fishing?" I asked.

LeRoy gave me a look that expressed I was a complete turd for asking such a thing. He replied with a sturdy, "No."

"Why not?"

LeRoy looked out the window and took a drag of his cigarette. "I only fish in the summer. I'm not fishing in the winter. Too cold. I'm not fishing in the winter. Nope, nope, nope, nope—"

"All right, man. No ice fishing. Jesus."

LeRoy made a handful of decisions based on the seasons. For instance, LeRoy only ate fruit in the summer. In his mind, I'm sure, it was asinine—or "gorilla horseshit"—that I would even question these seasonal decisions. (*Gorilla horseshit* being another amazing phrase uttered only from the lips of LeRoy Buchholz.)

It was quiet for a bit before LeRoy decided I was worthy enough to hear a more clarifying explanation about the ice fishing issue—an issue, it seemed, I had been completely ridiculous for leaning on him about. LeRoy told me a story of why he would never go on the ice again. It involved him driving with someone onto the frozen river and plopping down over a fishing hole. LeRoy didn't mind the cold, and it seemed to him that one had a tendency to catch more fish in the winter opposed to the summer. He said the fish were hungrier in the winter.

As he told the story—even after all these months together—those cynical synapses still fired in my brain, convincing me not to indulge LeRoy, not to believe this seemingly honest storyteller.

LeRoy continued to tell me he left his pole to rest in the hole and decided to wander off and take a look around, not putting too far a distance from his potential catch. While doing so, he came across some weak ice and crashed into the hypothermic waters of the Black River.

"I got out." He lit a cigarette. He inhaled real long, and he spoke in smoke, "I got out."

When I look back on these specific periods of time labeled by my dubiousness, I am embarrassed. I wonder if I had believed him, genuinely believed him, perhaps our relationship would have been even stronger. Maybe I could have escalated to some degree of confidant—who knows.

By the time he was done telling me the tale I didn't believe but pretended to, we arrived at the eye doctor. We walked through the parking lot, stopping by the doors so LeRoy could finish his smoke. We did not have to wait long in the little 1960s-brown waiting room before LeRoy was called in. I liked this eye doctor; he was an older optometrist in his sixties with white hair and fat glasses. He was friendly and treated LeRoy with kindness, often joking around with him. It was such an amazing and humbling scene to witness; there were these people in LeRoy's life who saw him and cared for him as I did, but they had been doing it for far longer than me.

"LeRoy, you get free frames, you know," he said.

"I know."

"If you know, then why don't you come in here and get them when your glasses break? I told you not to use the glue—it eats away at the frames. You're making them worse."

"Glue works fine," LeRoy argued.

"I'm just saying. Hey, what do you say we get you some new frames?"

"That's why I'm here," LeRoy said.

"No, I mean some *new* frames. Something a little more contemporary. Something a little more stylish for you."

"Nope. Nope. Nope," LeRoy stammered, shaking his head. "I like the ones I got. Just need my vision eyes."

The doctor stood up and patted LeRoy on the shoulder, smiling. "Whatever you want, LeRoy."

Because LeRoy had a standard prescription and frames, the doctor left for a bit and returned with a new pair of glueless, tapeless glasses, as if he had a whole closet of blocky, retro frames in the back specifically for these visits. LeRoy thanked him timidly, and the two of us headed back to his apartment.

Driving past the river, I was reminded of the story LeRoy told me an hour earlier, the ice fishing story I did not believe. As if he were reading my mind, LeRoy broke the silence once again.

"No one listens to me."

LeRoy would always say this, always made it a point to tell me no one ever listened to him. He would say this during the course of any conversation at any given time. It did not take much to trigger this reaction. After a while, when I began to take notice of LeRoy's interactions with the others—JB, Pug, Nate, Rob or Beth—a very heavy veil was lifted. It became very clear that most everybody was in fact not listening to him.

LeRoy would be cleaning the office, talking to one of the staff there, telling a story about how his bike got stolen for the fifth time (this did in fact happen) or how he fell through the ice on the Black River. Whomever he was speaking to would be reading the paper or shoveling high-calorie foods into an already swollen belly, patronizing him with *uh-huh*s and *you don't say*s. It was frustrating to witness.

LeRoy would be walking down the street, and he would make a comment about the weather, as he saw others do during cordial conversation. People would nod—or more times than not, put their heads down, ignoring him completely as they quickened their pace.

There were endless examples of this. But what it always came down to was LeRoy was right. As it would turn out, LeRoy was right most of the time, nearly all of the time. In the beginning, I did not believe him most of the time, and even this was just another example of someone not listening to him. It took much longer than I would have liked, but as we spent more time together, as time went on, as it got closer to the point when I was to leave him forever, I figured it out.

After that day at the eye doctor, driving back and forth past the Black River, I listened to every word that came out of LeRoy's mouth. I made it a point to believe him, regardless of how outlandish or fictitious his words came across. Toward the end of our time together, whenever LeRoy would complain no one was listening, I no longer ignored him or brushed off even these words as the products of an overly sensitive curmudgeon.

Instead I would simply tell him, "I know. But I do."

LeRoy would take a drag of his smoke, roll his eyes, and say, "Yeah, I guess *you* do."

I like to believe LeRoy knew I listened to him—that after some time, LeRoy knew I wasn't some guy who simply came in to make sure he was still alive so I could collect a paycheck. By now, I like to believe he knew, that he had to know, he and I were friends.

14

I didn't know why it hadn't crossed my mind before: I was driving the same vehicle in which LeRoy had sat next to me easily over a hundred times. Maybe it dawned on me then because I was so close to La Crosse. I involuntarily jerked my head to the right, thinking maybe for a second none of this had happened, maybe it was still 2004 and I was just having a blackout brought on by a night of drinking during Oktoberfest at Bodega. But no.

I looked through LeRoy's ghost to the passenger side window crank he had broken in an attempt to somehow get the window down even lower than when it completely recedes into the door. I had never got it fixed.

I was all at once nervous and excited. Excited to be back in La Crosse. Nervous because I felt as though I was somehow heading back to my time at CHCS, my time with LeRoy. I saw these impossible vignettes in my head of what it would be like when I saw him. What would I say? How would he look?

A shiver trickled upward through my whole body, like stepping out of a hot shower into a freezing bathroom. Maybe it was my body trying to get me back on track. I could not understand why my brain did not fully comprehend that in no time at all I *wasn't* going to be sitting across from LeRoy at Rosie's. I *wasn't* going to see what he looked like or have a conversation with him ever again. And I could not understand why my once-acute mind was now unable to tell me if I were sad or just embarrassed.

The only thing I did understand was that I was now in La Crosse for the first time in years—and I didn't have a fucking clue what I was going to do. I look back at the empty passenger seat and got caught up on the jiggling seat belt that protected no one.

There was much to learn about LeRoy's routines, and each new thing was as peculiar and intriguing as the next. One thing was more important than all else: LeRoy's cigarettes. LeRoy smoked nonstop—two to three packs a day. He smoked in his apartment, at Rosie's, outside his building, at numerous job sites, everywhere he was allowed.

LEROY

At our first meeting, JB told me LeRoy was not to smoke in anyone's vehicle, including mine. "Them's the rules," she said. This particular rule presented a bit of a conundrum: I smoked in my car pretty much any time I got in the damn thing, but LeRoy wasn't allowed to. The logical and fair reasoning would be that if LeRoy could not smoke in it, then I could not smoke in it.

Eventually, I came up with a bit of scheme. As it turned out, LeRoy also refused to wear his seat belt. There was a story behind this—a story you may remember from the beginning of the book. After that accident, LeRoy didn't want to wear a seat belt; according to him, it didn't matter. He had an unspoken agreement, unlike any other client at CHCS, that he did not have to wear his seat belt if he did not want to. During LeRoy's tenure at CHCS, no one had gotten him to wear one. No one but JB, of course, because LeRoy did whatever JB wanted, few questions asked. (And there was never "no questions asked" when it came to LeRoy.)

In the beginning, I tried to get him to wear one. It was a bit of a struggle. Whenever I brought up the issue, it usually led to a discussion about the accident ,and little bits and pieces of the blotchy, uneven story would be stretched out over long periods of time.

LeRoy did wear a seat belt without much resistance for a couple weeks after we had a near accident on I-90 and had to come to a very quick stop when he wasn't strapped in. Anticipating this sudden brake, I threw my arm across LeRoy's chest and braced both of us for any potential impact. I had to hold on to him pretty tightly. After that close call, LeRoy was a little freaked out. He wore his seat belt for a couple weeks until the posttraumatic stress wore off and he quit all together, going back to his old ways. Whenever he was wearing his seat belt, though, it was uncomfortable just to watch him. He acted as if he were being held down against his will. It looked as if he were letting his arch nemesis sit in his lap and smother him with a pillow.

After an afternoon of fishing on the Mississippi, LeRoy and I stopped at this tribal-owned gas station and smoke shop up on 16 to pick him up a carton of Winstons. It was a tobacco outlet of sorts, selling cartons of cheap cigarettes. It was here that I came up with the scheme. After purchasing a fairly cheap box of smokes, the two of us made our way back to the Jeep. I got his attention.

When he looked at me, I said, "Hey, LeRoy, you can smoke in my car if you wear your seat belt."

LeRoy paused and cautiously thought about the proposition I had just presented. He knew he wasn't supposed to smoke in anyone's car, and to top it off, JB was the one who had told him so. He was hesitant to go against anything JB said. To appease the man, I called JB right then and asked her permission—on LeRoy's behalf, of course.

"Well, uh, yeah," she agreed on the other end of the call. "If it gets him to wear his seat belt, that's fine. If it gets him to wear his seat belt," she repeated.

"It's okay by JB, LeRoy," I said as I hung up.

With that, LeRoy hopped right in. He examined the whole seat belt apparatus in its entirety—the Jeep's seat-belt-buckling process seemingly a completely foreign experience to him. He figured it out quickly, and in one majestic motion, buckled his seat belt and lit up a Winston simultaneously with quickness. It was as if he had four hands. This would be forever known as "The Day Dan Got LeRoy to Wear a Goddamn Seat Belt."

LeRoy and I would now had a new space to smoke together: my car. It was during these times that LeRoy and I had some of our most intimate talks, either while driving the winding roads of La Crosse or simply idling outside a CHCS house or his apartment.

As we pulled onto the freeway, leaving the gas station near Prairie Island where we purchased his cartons, we took the back way into Onalaska. The two of us settled in for a fifteen-minute trip to the big-ass house on Main Street.

As we headed toward the bridge on 90, LeRoy took a drag of his cigarette. Riding the smoke out of his mouth, he said, "I got hit there." He pointed out the rolled-down passenger window. (He always rolled the window down as far as it could go, severely testing the function of the hand-operated crank.) He motioned out ahead of us, out toward the shoulder.

"What the hell were you doing riding on the highway, man?"

"I can ride anywhere I want," he said, a little worked up—not in an angry way, just in the declarative way he said most things.

"All right, all right. Calm down," I said. "What happened?"

LeRoy lit another cigarette and sighed out the first drag. "I was ridin' down the street, and some guy opened his door while they drove down the street. The door hit me from behind, and I fell all over the goddamn place."

I pictured two redneck assholes driving down the freeway, laughing at the idea of knocking over a disabled guy on a bright red tricycle. Factoring the speed limit, the truck had to have been going at least forty-five miles per hour, unless these idiots had the decency (so hard to even use that word) to slow down before they hit him.

"Jesus, LeRoy. Were you okay?"

LeRoy kept pulling off the grit. "I don't remember. I just remember that my bike was broken and I walked home."

I did some quick logistic computing. We were a good five miles from LeRoy's apartment, if not farther. It would take hours to walk back to his place from there, even longer when one factors in his fierce and anchoring limp.

"Oh my God, LeRoy. That's horrible."

"It took me a while to get a new bike." The condition of his bike was clearly the most upsetting aspect of the situation as far as LeRoy was concerned.

That was the end of that story. He never brought it up again, and I would never hear anything further from anyone on the subject.

LeRoy just sat there, finishing his smoke, which he then put out in the palm of his baseball mitt of a hand. He placed the butt in the left front pocket of his shirt. I was appalled by this action. Without words, I pointed to the ashtray in the center console of the vehicle, an ashtray I had been known to use on more than one occasion.

Suddenly, LeRoy stretched himself into a perfectly prone position in the front seat, frantically searching in his pants pocket for something. His movements were so erratic, they were making me nervous. He was acting as if a clan of fire ants had made their home in his pants. He extended his whole body straight like this a few times in a row—it looked like precisely timed dosages of electric shock.

LeRoy whipped out a pack of Winstons from the newly purchased carton, and with an exhausted *"Humph,"* he sat back in a comfortable position in his seat. The electroshock treatment had been halted for now. He lit a smoke and asked me what we were doing today.

Not responding yet, I thought about these days we spent together. Remember Antoine's books? Well, LeRoy had books too, but instead of PX stores and Menucci's Pizzeria, his were populated with entries of Winston Shorts, Pall Mall Blues, and cheapo GPC smokes (which were quite disgusting). LeRoy would pick up packs of smokes anywhere—that was simple enough. But LeRoy would get his cartons at only two places, unless he was absolutely desperate. One was that tribal-owned gas station. We also hit up another stop over the bridge on Prairie Island, though rarely, due to the geographical perimeters of our usual stomping grounds. LeRoy would get a carton every two weeks, and anything else he'd have to buy on his own with his weekly allowances. I would buy him a pack about once a week whenever I picked some up for myself.

It took LeRoy a while to take the smokes from me. It was like trying to give a bone to a pup that hesitates to take what's offered because he's been tricked before. And on top of that, he knew he wasn't supposed to take gifts from any of the workers. No gifts. Not ever. This was the rule, and it was made clear to all of us right away.

But after a long while, there came a point when LeRoy and I were no longer just client and . . . whatever the hell you would call me—I would say we were friends. LeRoy was still cognizant of the fact that I was technically not allowed to give gifts, but he rolled with it. And despite the rules, LeRoy knew if he ran out of smokes four days before he could get a new carton, he would absolutely not be able make it. There was no way in hell he could go four days without a grit, so he would take what he could get when he could get it and from whomever he could get it.

Because of LeRoy's unflinching habit, he and I had to map out where to eat based upon whether he could smoke inside. We ate at only one place that didn't allow smoking: Ardie's, a nice little restaurant that didn't kill LeRoy's wallet. It's still on Highway 35 just south of I-90 on Lang Drive.

At a lot of the places we would go, LeRoy would get stiff looks—folks would always get uneasy around him. If he sneezed too loud and pulled out his handkerchief like a maniacal magician, management would come over and tell us to "keep it down," as if he were doing it on purpose, or they'd give our table a look that implied the same. But if I sneezed louder than normal, no one would bat an eye. This was truly a frustrating reality, but Ardie's was different. They were not like that at all. Ardie's was good people. They liked LeRoy and treated him as a regular who always paid and always had the same thing.

And like a regular, LeRoy had a specific table. It becomes clear while working with the cognitively disabled how much routine comforts them. Familiarity completely facilitates their daily life—they can control controllability to some degree. That is to say, by choosing to put themselves in comfortable environments, safe places, and safe situations they are familiar with, they establish little stress and generate some control. LeRoy was no exception to this rule. His spot at Ardie's was a dark wood booth with a tile and laminate top. It was almost all the way in the back on the left, next to a large window with a thick divider that blocked the view just enough to bug. There were only two booths behind it before the restaurant ended.

I asked LeRoy a hundred times why he sat there.

"I dunno. It's my table."

The staff would bring him coffee right away and would return shortly after with bottles of ketchup, mustard, and mayonnaise. These things—the coffee coupled with the specific condiments—were all comforting. LeRoy took refuge in these seemingly uninteresting, unimportant, and unconnected details. It was a sense of control and stability. It was his safe reality.

If LeRoy's table happened to be taken at Ardie's, he also had a backup booth. I don't recall where it was in the restaurant because we only sat at it once. On more than a couple occasions, he waved off the backup-booth option and said instead, "Let's go to Rosie's."

And then we come back to the infamous Rosie's Cafe. Now *this* is a place to eat. LeRoy loved this place, and so did I. LeRoy and I had our booth and a backup booth and a backup booth for the backup booth. Hell, sometimes LeRoy would even choose to sit at the little bar with the short, red-vinyl-topped stools.

When we sat down, our coffee was filled right away and an ashtray dropped in front of our faces. I got the same thing every time: the mushroom Swiss burger. And for LeRoy, a fish sandwich (he had a love of tartar sauce that I found off-putting) with the soup of the day. Let it be known he was known to order the mushroom Swiss as well from time to time.

Rosie's was not much to look at, but they had a mushroom Swiss burger that was simply the best—out of this fucking world. The lovely ladies of Rosie's, in their jeans and T-shirts wrapped in aprons, were always flashing smiles. This had to be the key. A Buddhist lama once told me food tastes better when prepared by a happy chef—to never eat food prepared by an angry chef. And let me tell you, there were no angry chefs at Rosie's.

LeRoy would mix his condiments together—the ketchup, mustard, and mayonnaise—and dip his fries and sandwich in it. It was absolutely disgusting. When he got his coffee, LeRoy added six sugars and some salt and stirred it with his index finger, smoking like a bastard all the while. No one at Rosie's ever gave LeRoy a hard time either; not one dirty look, not a scoff, no assumptions he was going to cause a ruckus. So we would go in twice, sometimes three times a week, eat our food, smoke our grits, and drink our coffee. I would steal LeRoy's pickle, and for five minutes he would play along until he got annoyed and flashed me his *that's enough* look. We enjoyed it there. Rosie's never got old.

LeRoy would also often eat at home; after all, he could always smoke there. Recall JB's warning about eating anything he cooked himself? Well, it would become apparent through conversation that LeRoy could not see the difference about eating hamburger raw versus eating it cooked. I mean, he knew there was a difference between cooked and uncooked meat, of course, but he thought it silly. He never said it upset his tummy one way or the other, so what was the problem?

"Who needs to cook?" LeRoy told me once as I watched him put a pile of raw hamburger in the microwave. It had to be over a pound. He cooked it for three minutes and dug in immediately as it came out of the micro. It was clearly not even close to being in a safely consumable state. "I get my food when I need it," he said. "Rosie's is better anyway."

CHCS gave him a hot plate once, but he started a fire. So the story goes. This was another incident relayed to me by those who knew LeRoy long before I had. The fire was nothing serious, but the hot plate became a liability nonetheless.

LeRoy did not start the fire because he was not paying attention or because he was not trained in the operation of the hot plate. His reaction time just wasn't up to par. LeRoy's balance and reflexes were also real issues, maybe *the* issues. He would knock things over, and his depth perception was almost always off unless he was bowling or on the bocce ball court. (His Special Olympics medals more than vouched for that.)

LeRoy usually went into story mode and started describing one of his accidents as a point of reason for his discombobulation. "It's because of when I went through that windshield, you know. If it had been any closer, I would have died." Or he would say, "It's because when I fell off the bluff, you know." LeRoy never used his accidents as excuses, just simply explanations.

Besides eating and smoking, LeRoy and I filled our time with day-to-day errands. There was the lawn mowing, of course, the office cleaning, and the fishing. We bowled together often, or sometimes I would drop him off at the alley one to three times a week. There was bocce ball in the summer and consulting with the *TV Guide* to figure out when to watch *Gunsmoke*. We went shopping for one thing or another almost every day. There were so many things I had to get accustomed to—but there was LeRoy, guiding me through the whole crazy goddamn thing. I didn't help LeRoy with every little thing, though. For instance, I rarely, if ever, helped him with laundry or groceries. I knew Nate and Pug did that a lot with him.

Pug was an athletic kid with good posture and

shaved-to-a-shine head. His nickname derived from the first three letters of his last name, and everyone called him by this sobriquet—except LeRoy. LeRoy called him only Matt. I first met Pug during our freshman year. He and the other friends I made that first year were all Wisconsinites who had gone to high school together in Waukesha. In our sophomore year, I got to know Pug even more after we all moved into that derelict duplex together.

Pug took LeRoy grocery shopping and helped him with his laundry—basically all the things I did not do with him. He handled some of LeRoy's meals too. They would hit up Rosie's sometimes, although not nearly as much as LeRoy and I did. He also brought LeRoy to bocce and bowling practice every once in a while.

When I left for New Mexico, Pug took over my LeRoy duties completely. I would call him from Santa Fe, asking how LeRoy was doing, and Pug would relay the tales of typical LeRoy awesomeness. I knew LeRoy was in good hands with him, but eventually Pug too had to leave La Crosse. And then there were two worried minds concerned about LeRoy's well-being.

I also often thought about those who had worked with LeRoy in the past. How many "Dans" had come before me, and how many did LeRoy take a liking to? It was a thought I had regularly, but I never asked LeRoy about these Dans. It was another mysterious part of LeRoy's life best left to LeRoy.

LEROY

Don't get me wrong. As much mystery as there was surrounding LeRoy, there were constants, many constants—the most prevalent being watching *Gunsmoke* and driving in my Jeep together, both of us chain-smoking, and me answering LeRoy's ever-repeating question, "What are we doing today?"

At that moment, I realized I still hadn't answered LeRoy from when he asked that very question earlier. We were on our way to mow lawns, of course, and I told him this through a thick screen of cigarette smoke and humidity that snuck in through the open windows—LeRoy's more than mine. Whether he even realized it was the answer to a question he asked minutes ago, LeRoy seemed satisfied.

To understand LeRoy, take Antoine as another example: Antoine seemed to see his life as an abyss, an abyss he was falling through, just waiting to smash to the bottom. I thought Antoine felt this nothingness every single day with only small vignettes of hope and happy anxiousness. I strongly believe Antoine felt everything he did was futile, from his first bite of Menucci's mushroom-and-sausage pizza to his last shaky scratch of his lottery tickets.

But LeRoy, through small flashes of brilliance, every great once in a while, had an idea of what kind of hand he had been dealt, and he used it to his advantage as best he could. Futility was not something LeRoy Buchholz believed in, let alone practiced.

So much of my drive was filled with memories and interruptions, by the time I actually reached La Crosse, the four and a half-hour drive I had been grumbling over the entire way didn't feel so long at all. And now that I was back in LAX, I felt afraid for some reason, and wished I had hours more to drive.

As I drove into town I caught a billboard boasting Elvis impersonators which made my anxiousness dissipate, and a smile immediately replaced whatever sour expression preceded it. I don't have an explanation for it, but there seemed to be an out-of-place connection between Elvis Presley and La Crosse, Wisconsin, perhaps due to a bit of town lore that involved Elvis playing a show there on May 14th, 1956. A show that was so "overtly sexual," it prompted the local newspaper to complain to FBI director, J. Edgar Hoover. Obviously I wouldn't know anything about this intimately due to its taking place twenty eight years before I was born, but man . . . I think I had known someone once who might have been able to shine some light on it.

"I knew Elvis," LeRoy said as he sat across from me at our booth at Rosie's. "I knew Elvis, and I told him to quit taking drugs. I told him to quit taking drugs 'cause I told him it would kill him."

The words out of his mouth took a moment to register in my brain, an action discernible by the slow chewing of my mushroom Swiss burger at seven o'clock in the morning. The thing about LeRoy was that there was never any buildup to what he said. We were talking about the lawns that had to be mowed that day, then we were eating in complete silence, then BAM! Out of nowhere, he was telling me about his relationship with Elvis Presley.

LeRoy's words amalgamated in my brain, stewing together into one congealed mass of *what?* My chewing slowed until it stopped altogether. Mushrooms, ground beef, and Swiss cheese were now just sitting in a ball in the back of my mouth.

I waved at the thick curtain of smoke LeRoy dropped in front of me. "What?" I stopped waving. "*What?*"

"Yep," LeRoy went on. "I told him to quit taking those drugs. Drugs'll kill you. Sure enough, he died later on after we talked. I saw it. I saw it."

"What the hell are you talking about?" Well into my relationship with LeRoy at this point, I had long since determined to not only listen to everything he said but to trust him emphatically. Still, I couldn't help but think he *knew* I had talked myself into that rule and was now just fucking with me—testing me. "You saw him? How did you know Elvis?" I paused for minute. "You are talking about *Elvis*, Elvis, right?

"Elvis," LeRoy repeated.

"Elvis *Died-Taking-a-Shit* Presley?"

LeRoy, apparently unfamiliar with my uncouth reference, kept smoking, looking confused before coyly smiling at my use of the word *shit*.

"How did you tell him all this?" I asked.

"On the phone. On the phone I told him," he clarified.

"You talked to Elvis Presley on the phone?" I could not hide my skepticism.

LeRoy lit a new cigarette before his other was finished and signaled to one of the three waitresses wandering around that he needed a coffee refill. His way of doing this was particularly unique: In the booth, he would half-stand, half-crouch as if he had a cramp in his butt. Slightly bent over, he would raise his right arm as high as he could with his index finger extended to the sky. He would not specify what he needed exactly, but rather would utter half words, like when Kramer on *Seinfeld* was riled up and trying to explain something to Jerry. Rosie saw him and nodded the way she always did, letting LeRoy know she'd get him his coffee. LeRoy crashed back down in his seat and picked up right where I left off. "Yeah, a couple times," he said.

I did my best to keep up. "You talked to Elvis on the phone—a couple times—and told him to quit taking drugs?"

"Yep, I told him to quit taking drugs, but he didn't listen to me. He's dead. He should have listened to me, right?"

I shook my head. I couldn't help but immediately assume he was confused about who this Elvis actually was. But I wanted to hear more about this craziness, so I replied, "Yeah, LeRoy, he should have listened to you."

My hope was that LeRoy would get deeper into the story—and quickly. At times, it took him a while to get things out, especially if he sensed the other person was overtly interested in what he had to say—a rare occurrence, I imagine.

As LeRoy staggered through his next words, I grew impatient and was no longer able to hold back my arsenal of questions. "How did you get his phone number?" I began.

"He knew me," he said. "I knew him, and he gave it to me. He gave it to me."

"He gave it to you?" I asked, painfully wanting to get to the bottom of this ridiculous exclamation.

"Yeah . . . he gave it to me, Dan. Sheesh!" As far as I can remember, this was the first time LeRoy ever called me by name in a statement directed specifically at me.

The time passed the story more than the story passed the time, and by its end, I had brushed it off as nonsense, nothing but a silly LeRoyism. I had sincerely failed at keeping my promise of always believing him no matter what. But who could blame me? I mean, c'mon—*LeRoy and Elvis Presley*?

LeRoy told a lot of stories. However, the fascinating thing was that the stories he told me were never proven *wrong* per se. Many parts of his stories would show up later in documents or conversations with others. For instance, I never believed he lived in the woods, like a Sasquatch, until other people at CHCS confirmed it. Other parts of stories were just never confirmed 100 percent, but still never proven wrong.

We were in the car once when LeRoy told me about the rape he stopped from his apartment window—another tale I figured to be tall. I was later proven wrong when I saw the medal on his wall and Rob spoke of it in passing. I also don't think I would have believed the story of his car accident, if it had not heard it first from JB. In retrospect, I don't know what caused me to be so untrusting of his stories. When I look back on it, I feel embarrassed and ashamed of my cynicism.

But I was not the only one who held these disbeliefs. When I was driving to a demo job with Rob, I brought up this Elvis conversation I had had with LeRoy at Rosie's. With one hand on the wheel of his old red beater Dodge pickup, Rob smiled hard and laughed without sound as I retold the conversation. He nodded his head along with the Rolling Stones' *Sticky Fingers* album crackling through the truck's blown-out speakers.

"Yeah, I've heard that one too," he said. "Frickin' Buchholz, man."

Rob was extraordinary. Seriously awesome. During my time at CHCS and also while working with those incredible students at Burnsville, I came into contact with only a few people who really loved this kind of work. I've come to realize only a select few really belong in this kind of work, and it resonates in their attitude and behavior toward those they work with. So many people are uneducated and impatient with the mentally disabled, but shockingly, some of these individuals work right alongside the ones who do understand. There are folks in this line of work who really should have nothing to do with people like LeRoy and Antoine—let alone be responsible for their well-being. It's these people, like Dumbshit, who simply do not understand the mind. But the people who get it, who excel at this work, understand the mind as well as the individual, and they understand these are not mutually exclusive components. These are people like Shelden, JB, Nate, Pug (another roommate who also worked with LeRoy), Beth, and Jolene. And especially Rob.

LeRoy had much respect for Rob. Rob was LeRoy's favorite and rightfully so; you could see it every time they were together. They acted like brothers, teasing each other, listening to each other, and believing each other—always. Rob never became impatient with or tired of LeRoy, no matter how bizarre or frustrating he may have been. I might have been jealous of their relationship, a relationship I pushed too hard for myself with LeRoy.

Rob reminded me to keep my mind constantly open—not by telling me, but by showing me. He acted this way with every client. No matter what house we went to, no matter what day, everyone became excited, ignoring whatever it was they doing. They all loved Rob. He would walk into those houses like Brad Pitt walking into the Ivy. They all admired him so much. Rob was their hero. They all wanted him to pay attention to them; they all wanted to talk to him, ask him questions, and tell him about their lives, regardless of how minute the details. They all wanted to tell him what they were doing that day, what they had done the night before, and what they were planning to do tomorrow.

Working with Rob five days a week, as I did in

the summer months, kept me completely in check. He repeatedly showed me how to transcend merely working with these individuals. I learned you have to make their needs and their lives a part of your own. Even though we were encouraged to leave work at the door, heroic individuals such as Rob are unable to do that—this is the difference. They make it a part of their life. It has to be more than a job for them.

There was something else that bound Rob and LeRoy together, something I could never compete with: Rob's two-year-old daughter, Emma. She was little and cute and smelled good, like most babies do. LeRoy felt an intense affinity toward her, some rare connection.

Whenever she was around, he would get real close to her, right up in her face, and whisper, "Uncle LeRoy . . . Can you say, '*Unnnncle* LeRoy'?" "Uncle" was drawn out long and "LeRoy" was quick and squeaky. Emma would giggle and smile.

Rob and his wife trusted LeRoy and even let him hold her. I imagine not too many people would allow someone in LeRoy's "condition" to hold their fragile baby daughter, but LeRoy would lie in traffic for that child. No question.

From time to time, the three of us would make pit stops at Rob's house to pick up tools or wood, and LeRoy would always sneak in to see Emma. If the three of us needed to do work at Rob's house, LeRoy would take "Emma breaks" instead of smoke breaks. We would be outside working on some task or another, and I would hear LeRoy speaking from inside the house in a cartoonish, high-pitched voice. I would always hear laughter, LeRoy's and Emma's, immediately following this voice.

When it was nearing the end of my time with LeRoy, Rob and I were called in one morning to thoroughly clean LeRoy's apartment, which included repainting it. You see, LeRoy received money from the state so he could live in the apartment and buy food and other amenities. But that meant the state would come to his apartment two times a year to make sure he was using the money properly and living in a clean and sanitary environment.

Now, LeRoy mostly lived in a sanitary environment, but the walls of his apartment were stained an odd yellow from the smoke, and he wasn't the tidiest of tenants. LeRoy's apartment reminded me of my dad's parent's house. It was little more than an olfactory memory—they lived at that house when I was a little guy, five or so. But LeRoy's apartment had that same smell as their house, that kind of smokiness. The furniture and countertops were saturated with the old sweetness of tobacco. I liked it.

But for inspection, Rob and I had to clean what LeRoy dirtied. This was no easy task—it took days. We cleaned the place as if he were moving out of it. We washed the floors, vacuumed relentlessly, and cleaned the fridge (which LeRoy hated us doing). We also de-Sassied the apartment—removed all her matted fur from the carpet and furniture and cleaned her up a bit the best we could. (She took after her dad and did not like to be cleaned up.)

The day before the inspection, Rob was out getting more paint (he did most, if not all, of the painting) with LeRoy, and I was left in the apartment alone. I entered the forbidden zone: LeRoy's room. There was not much to do in there, as there was not much in the room to begin with. The walls were mostly bare. A massive chain hung above his bed with over a dozen Special Olympics gold and silver medals for bocce ball and bowling. On another wall hung a framed certificate. The story behind the certificate took place well before I ever arrived in La Crosse.

LeRoy always slept in his work clothes. Every now and then he would keep his boots off at least, but many of the times I walked in on him sleeping I'd see the boots on and laced up. That way, if he had to get up quickly for any reason, he would be dressed and ready to go. This habit came in handy one early morning when LeRoy heard a commotion out his window. He looked out and saw a man assaulting a woman. Completely dressed, he ran to the phone and called the cops, then hurried as fast as he could down to the alley and started yelling at the guy. LeRoy scared off the assailant, and the cops were able to catch him running away from the alley. It seemed LeRoy had stopped a rape from taking place, and the cops gave him a certificate of honor, a framed accomplishment he hung proudly in his bare bedroom.

The one thing I did have to check out in his bedroom was his closet, which I discovered to be packed full of random shit. It felt strange to be in there. I felt as if this were the only private place LeRoy had, and here I was, going through it like some tidy-obsessed parent. As I cleaned and tried my best to organize all of LeRoy's things that resided inside the small accordion-doored space, I eventually came across a large pile of clothes LeRoy had worn only once, if at all. I had never personally seen LeRoy wear any of these articles. Just as I was about to tackle this mighty heap, I heard the front door open and LeRoy's jingling ass come in.

He hollered for me. "Dan!"

"I'm in here," I shouted.

LeRoy stuck his head in through the door. "Smoke break?"

"LeRoy, you're in your own home. There's no such thing in here. You can smoke whenever you want."

"We're working!" he squealed before turning around.

"Wait!" I said before he could leave. I pulled out a pair of trousers from the closet and showed them to LeRoy. "Will you wear these?"

"Nope."

I pulled out a couple shirts, perfectly pressed.

"Will you wear these?"

"Nope." LeRoy shook his head no with a cigarette in his mouth.

I kept digging until there was nothing left but what looked to be old Folgers Coffee cans. But shit, were they heavy. I lifted the lid to the first of six cans, and I could not believe what I saw. I opened the other five immediately. Each can was filled to the brim with change—mostly quarters.

"Holy shit, LeRoy! Get back in here!"

LeRoy walked back into the room. "What?"

"There has to be—I don't know—a couple hundred dollars in these cans."

"What?" LeRoy asked without looking at me, not knowing what I was clambering about.

A smile took over my face, as if I had discovered a treasure under the floorboards of my own apartment. "Come here. Sit down here."

LeRoy sat down painfully, his hips rigid and unforgiving. I showed him each coffee can filled with change. Keep in mind LeRoy was kind of obsessed with money. He always wanted as much money as he could have, so you can imagine my surprise at these coffers of riches. I emptied the first can on the carpeted floor, and I was yet again shocked and excited to see so much money just from this one can. I figured there could be about five hundred dollars in all six cans combined.

LEROY

"LeRoy, we can go get this cashed. You can have five hundred dollars to spend on whatever you want."

LeRoy jumped up so quickly, he startled me and knocked over one of the cans, spilling change everywhere.

"What's wrong, LeRoy?" I asked nervously.

He was acting stranger than normal, stranger than I had ever seen. He started pacing in the bedroom, back and forth, agitated and serious as death. He patted himself for a cigarette, found one, lit it, and started smoking it really fast, even for LeRoy.

"*No*! That's not for me. That's not for me. That money is not mine."

This made me even more nervous. Initially, I thought maybe LeRoy had stolen the money without knowing the severity of the act, but that was so unlike him. He was never known to steal anything other than gasoline fumes.

"What, LeRoy? *What*?" I was almost scared now.

"When Emma was born, I started saving money for her."

I was overwrought with an indescribable feeling of goodness, but not for something I had done. I could not believe what I was hearing. "LeRoy, what are you talking about?"

"This money is for Emma . . . I've been saving this for her. I want her to have a good life. That's Emma's money. I want her to have whatever she wants."

I was dumfounded, then sad, then completely touched. I was amazed—everything I had ever thought about LeRoy was realigned and brightened.

"You can't give it to her yet. I'm not done yet," LeRoy said, panicked.

Shit. Not only had he been saving his money for years, but he wasn't even done yet. I looked at LeRoy and gave him one of my cigarettes, a Parliament Light. LeRoy didn't like these, but he took it anyway and lit it up. I put my hand on his shoulder and knocked my head against his, from which he pulled away quickly but without anger.

"LeRoy, you're something else, man. Emma will be so grateful."

LeRoy took a drag of my Parliament and told me he liked it, compensating for not liking it much at all. LeRoy smiled, and without touching me, he said, "No one gets that money but Emma."

I put the canisters back in their place. I moved an old pile of mail from the closet shelf to the floor, and as I did, something fell out of the yellow, coffee-stained pile of forgotten rubbish. It appeared to be an old photograph with indecipherable writing on the back; the ink had smeared and faded from years of being shuffled about. I leaned back on my sandaled heels, and all hunkered down, I flipped the photograph over.

There staring back at me was a photograph of a very young LeRoy and a very real Elvis Presley.

16

I was finally in LAX. I rolled in on 90, past the initial outskirt hotels that straddle La Crosse and Onalaska. I was giddy and nervous and sad, and I anticipated something that felt grand, but I had no idea what it was. I suppose I was ultimately confused.

It's hard to explain what arriving in La Crosse felt like this particular time. Every time I had come back, it had been a supremely positive experience. And even though I was coming back under such soul-crushing circumstances, I was still happy to be back—and the only immediate emotion I could gather was straight-up guilt.

If I am one thing, it is nostalgic, nearly to a fault. I can't help but think I was unable to separate all the wonderfully positive feelings I associated with LeRoy with this one and only shitty part—his death. I tried to shake that nastiness as I drove past the VFW, where we gorged ourselves on Wisconsin fish fry. I caught the top of Granddad Bluff off in the distance, which reminded me both of the excited, stoned hikes the boys and I took in the warmer months as well as one of LeRoy's worst accidents. Seeing these same places caused exciting, happy memories lightly glazed with dark ones.

I drove past a few of the CHCS houses as I rounded corners that would bring me to La Crosse Street and eventually the east end of campus. Driving past campus was the only time I didn't think about LeRoy's passing. Instead, it brought back memories of four perfect years of learning, relationships, and, for lack of a better term, fun.

So there I was, back in my most favorite city in a crucial battle over my own most base emotions: happiness versus sadness.

After I had graduated from La Crosse and headed south to New Mexico, I could not wait to get back. Not because I wasn't happy in Santa Fe—quite the contrary. La Crosse just held so many essential, life-changing experiences for me, so going back was always a satisfying trip of time travel. I had gone back three or four times before, but I never would have thought the most meaningful trip back would follow LeRoy's death. To be honest, I had never once thought of him dying.

LEROY

Driving through La Crosse brought back all sorts of intense feelings of nostalgia. I drove past the Diamond Way Buddhist Center I occupied for some months. Rosie's was only a minute or so down the road. Nothing had changed; it was still perfect. It was stupid, but I felt as if it had been waiting for me to come back. I could have stayed forever in that moment, never gone back, stayed in La Crosse for the rest of my life.

I pulled up along the curb across the street from the diner. There was almost no one inside—maybe one or two of the old-time regulars. It was like walking into a time portal.

The first time I started to really see LeRoy—that is, when I realized he was letting me witness the realness of him—we happened to be sitting at our booth at Rosie's. Our booth was the smallest in the place. It was crammed up against the wall, next to the second entrance/fire exit behind the horseshoe diner bar.

We were sitting at that booth, our booth, when LeRoy let out a big cough, a table-shaking *ahem*. He pulled out his handkerchief, a blue-and-white bandana classic he always carried in his back right pocket. He excused himself from the table and started to wobble on outside. It was clear early on that bodily functions embarrassed LeRoy, from nose blowing to farts. So when he was in a public space and had to blow his nose, he would remove himself altogether and partake in that action alone elsewhere. If he farted, which was never on purpose, the embarrassment clouded his motherboard, and he could not quite collect his thoughts for some few minutes.

I addressed this idiosyncrasy as he was getting up from the table. "LeRoy, you don't have to excuse yourself—it's fine."

LeRoy shook his head and mumbled some incomprehensible sounds as he limped his way through and out the door. LeRoy wobbled out and rested his broken body against this archaic industrial pipe erected to act as a railing. It really was just a pipe: gray, almost blue; smooth with six ringed grooves that screwed into an identical twin pipe.

I was turned around, arms crossed with my elbows buoying and bouncing for control over the back of my seat. I watched LeRoy through the large "Rosie's" etched across the front window. He propped all his weight onto the pipe and blew his nose into the blue-and-white bandana furiously for several long seconds. He stopped, sighed a heavy sigh, and then simply rested. LeRoy repeated this action once or twice more, staring out into the bluffs in the distance at times, but mostly just across the street.

At first I thought he was just staring off, thinking about what he was going to eat later or maybe trying to memorize my name or Pug's. But he was not thinking of any of these things. He was staring at the respectable red brick house with the white garage door that sat directly across the street from Rosie's diner.

LeRoy was memorizing a scene. He was memorizing a life where he stands in the front yard, watering the huge deciduous bushes overshadowing the house and its front bay windows, which are far too big, also dwarfing the house. He was memorizing a scene where he fixes his bike in the driveway. It is turned upside down on its handle bars and seat, which is wrapped in a towel so it does not get scuffed up. He greases the chain and spins the pedals in a large circle to make the wheels go. He was memorizing the order in which he adds more wires and trinkets to the frame and the basket, which has been detached so it doesn't crush on the asphalt beneath the weight of his bike. LeRoy likes the driveway—it is quiet. He can work there undisturbed without any assholes looking at him, snickering and making jokes, calling him "retard" and "faggot."

He was memorizing the scene where he lives in that house, just him and Sassy, and his friends Dan and Pug stop by to say hello and to grill up some burgers. He grills a hamburger on a Weber grill I have just helped him put together. He tells me he could have done it on his own and that I have done it wrong. I try to teach him how to do all the grilling stuff, how to cook the meat, but the whole time, LeRoy tells me he already knows how to do it.

It was this scene he had been staring at, with me just staring at him. It was impossible even for me to not see LeRoy in these doppelgänger realities. I know it seems silly to get so wrapped up in a fantasy, but I couldn't help it. If anything, it kept me thinking he would be okay after I left, even though his being okay had nothing to do with me.

Near the very end of my time with LeRoy, after we had discussed my moving from La Crosse to someplace far away, we sat at Rosie's one early Saturday morning eating our burgers. Mushroom Swiss burgers were often our first meal of the day—you could order them as early as 5:00 am. LeRoy's back faced the entrance. He turned around and pointed to the house across the street, the house with the bushes and the invisible upside-down bike.

"I could live in a house." He paused. "I could live in that house."

I chewed on my burger, nodding along in agreement with LeRoy's dream.

"Do I have enough money in my account to get that house over there?" he asked.

It's hard to describe what I felt when I heard him say this. It wasn't shocking, nor did it throw me off my duty, but I was aware that something—maybe even more than something—was on the line with how I was going to reply. So I thought it best not to. I nodded slowly, but not too slowly, and reached across the table to spark the unlit cigarette that bobbed on his lips. "We'll just have to see, LeRoy."

That seemed to suffice for this particular conversation. But that would not be the only day LeRoy would ask if he had enough money in his account, a checking account that rarely rose above five hundred dollars. It was a question so couched in hope. And whenever he asked, it would remind me of who LeRoy truly was and how his mind really worked.

I could spend day after day with LeRoy, and his cognitive disability would disappear completely. It would just be like hanging out with a buddy, with one of my roommates. And then he would ask about the house, and this devilish veil of normalcy would lift, revealing the realm of LeRoy's own reality, where confusion reigned and logic was ephemeral.

It was just so fucking sad. It was painful to hear. It was a hard shock that depressed me, no matter how hard I tried to let it go or downplay it. All it did was make me want to help LeRoy get that house somehow, even though it never went up for sale during our time together.

Each time, I wanted to look at LeRoy with a confident smile and be able to say with all truthfulness that he did in fact have enough money in his account to buy the little house across the street from Rosie's diner. Unfortunately, this was an answer I could never give him. This was something I knew could never be done. No matter how hard either of us wished it, with the exception of some act of God—a God neither LeRoy nor I believed in—he would never occupy that house.

Whenever LeRoy asked me his question there in our booth, he would lean in real close, with one blackened, chapped, rosacea-camouflaged elbow propped on Rosie's shiny Formica tabletop, with his eyebrows raised, waiting for a positive response—a hopeful yes.

But I could only shake my head in what felt like some trite, no-other-option response. When you know the absolute answer is no, yet you simply cannot bring yourself to say that—it's absolutely devastating. I felt like a fraud. I'd light up another cigarette and repeat my mantra every time: "We'll just have to see, brother. We'll just have to see."

With this response, LeRoy would slouch back, ignoring my answer, perhaps embarrassed or annoyed by this twenty-one-year-old nobody's indirectness. LeRoy always picked up on my stifling passiveness, but that would never deter his questioning. By now, LeRoy was most certainly used to my parry—as well as the disappointment that accompanied it. But he seemed to no longer allow it to affect him.

As with everything else, LeRoy had an amazing way of making it all okay. I think he understood his reality. And although he was surely disappointed each time, LeRoy would take a deep breath and sigh it all out while he slumped back into our booth, hard. With the slightest shrug, he'd attempt to get eye contact with the waitress. He'd hold up his index finger, stained with yellow indicators of decades of smoking, and give a simple head nod, signaling the waitress, letting her know he needed a refill on his coffee: black with six sugars and sometimes a shake or two of salt.

17

The snow had slowed some, but not much. I hadn't checked the weather report before leaving, and now I wondered if I would be stuck here in a Wisconsin winter storm. I supposed I would know soon enough.

I sat at Rosie's, still relishing in how little La Crosse had changed since I was last here. Getting to Rosie's was as easy as it had been years before—there were no new routes to learn. I thought it funny how such a small thing as sitting at our old table could make me so goddamn happy. It felt as if I had been gone only a day.

Rosie wasn't working, but her daughter was, and she came right over. I ordered a cup of coffee and asked for an ashtray. When she left, I took my writing pad out of my bag and started scribbling down memories from here and there—nothing specific. She returned quickly with the items. I lit a cigarette and sipped my coffee. After a little while, I stopped writing and pulled out my recorder. Hoping the batteries wouldn't run out while I was there (and that no one would think I was too crazy, talking into a small recorder they couldn't see), I started in on another story of LeRoy.

The phone rang at a quarter after five in the morning. The year was 2004, and my roommates and I were not that cell phone crazy yet. Not everyone was dependent on them in 2004, at least not in our house. We had a landline downstairs. For some reason, on that particular predawn, I could barely hear the ring. And I figured if I couldn't hear it, then no one else really could, so I let it go to the machine. When the machine picked up, whoever was calling hung up immediately, so I rested comfortably under my covers, squinting through my drapes to see the reassuring haze of early morning.

I was just about to fall back asleep when the phone rang again.

"Goddammit, Dmo, get the phone—you know it's for you," Carl shouted from the bottom of the steps.

I got up and walked down the short hallway with one bedroom to my left, one bedroom to my right, and a bathroom dead ahead. I stopped at the top of the steps and shouted back to Carl, "You're already down there. Just pick it up!"

"You just pick it up!"

Now, most of you don't know Carl that well or at all, so let me fill you in that I've cut this scene down by fifteen minutes or so. Carl and I would often yell back and forth in this very same manner while the telephone would keep ringing and going to the machine, during which time either one of us could have answered it half a dozen times. As this was going on that particular morning, Nate and Matt awoke, angry and groggy, yelling at both Carl and me—not placing the blame on either one of us specifically but rather equally annoyed with the both of us. The phone rang again. Finally, I high-stepped down our two flights of steps, shoulder-popped Carl as he smiled his dickface smile, found the phone in the screened-in porch, and I grabbed the receiver off its cradle. I realized I had not heard the phone all that well because, for some reason beyond my comprehension, it was out on the frigid, drafty porch I used for my smoke breaks.

"Yeah, what?" I barked.

"I'm going to call the police. I need to call the police."

"Who the hell is this?"

"I'm going to call the police," the mystery man's voice told me again.

It was this second repetition of the police threat that gave me a moment to wake up a bit and recognize the man on the other end.

"Who is this?" I asked LeRoy quietly and sarcastically. "You know it's Saturday, right? What did we talk about us sleeping in on Saturdays?"

"I'm calling the police!" His tone now went from normal to agitated. He was nervous. He was scared.

"Calm down! Hold on!"

I changed my own tone, trying to relax the frantic voice on the other end of the line as I pulled the porch door shut behind me. I grabbed Carl's coat off our butcher block table, which was actually just a stand for our FryDaddy, as I tried to bundle up unsuccessfully due to my lack of pants.

"LeRoy, listen to me," I told him. "Absolutely under no circumstances are you to call the police. I'm coming over right now."

I threw some pants on, got in the Jeep, and checked the time. It was 5:29 am. It usually took me about seven minutes to get to LeRoy's if I hit every light and sped a little, which was something I did not like to do.

All the elderly tenants at LeRoy's apartment building had been up for, like, three hours already. They waved as I walked in, said hello, and wished me a good morning, no longer seeing me as the youth threat they had for so long. I trudged through the sea of grandchildren stories, complaints about the inedible food and government, and litanies of the medicines they were ingesting that week. Once I made it through the old-person obstacle course, I passed up the elevator (being sure not to chance my speed by taking that staggeringly old piece of shit) and went directly up the four flights of stairs to LeRoy's apartment, taking three at a time. I fumbled with my keys, attempting to unlock the door myself and get in there before he haphazardly called the police. I went in without knocking—something I had never done before. And when I stormed through the door, I found LeRoy sitting at the kitchen table, smoking a cigarette with TV Land on. A preview for *My Three Sons* was blaring in the background. I was out of breath and nearly doubled over after making it from my bedroom to LeRoy's apartment in eleven minutes. It would have been even sooner if I had not needed to cross the arc of time downstairs.

"Are you okay?" I asked, still trying to catch my breath. As I pulled in huge breaths, I inhaled copious amounts of the secondhand smoke filling the room and making it even harder to recover air.

LeRoy jumped out of his chair. At first I thought it was because I had entered without knocking and I had startled him, but he paid me no attention as he limped into the living room faster than I had ever seen him move before. LeRoy picked up his vacuum, lifting it high with his left hand. It was nearly too heavy for him, and he almost toppled over. He was trying to hold it over his head with one arm but was unable to do so. With his cigarette burning at the filter, he yelled through pursed lips and a long ash, "See!"

As it turned out, LeRoy had been vacuuming at about four in the morning, which was something completely normal for LeRoy to do. While completing his early-morning chore, the vacuum began smoking, then immediately started on fire. LeRoy had put out the fire with a nearby cup of coffee and had left the vacuum sitting in the exact spot—a small puddle of murky, caffeinated water.

"LeRoy, put the vacuum down."

LeRoy obliged hesitantly and placed the vacuum on the ground as gently as he could with one arm. I walked over to him and squatted down next to the vacuum cleaner. He exited the living room, sat back down at the kitchen table, and lit up another grit.

"Good thing you showed up," LeRoy told me. "I was just about to call the police."

"No you weren't."

"Oh yes I was."

Realizing I was not going to win this one, I flipped the vacuum over and checked out the situation. Upon further investigation, I discovered a tangled mass of fishing line and broken pieces of casting lures had wrapped themselves around the roller, made their way up into the canister, heated thoroughly, and caused the fire.

An avid fisherman, LeRoy had tackle and fishing

line all over the apartment. Ignoring this very obvious fact, LeRoy was convinced someone had broken into his apartment while he was sleeping and intricately wrapped fishing line around the motor of the vacuum—not to mention broke his lures and shoved those in the vacuum—to "sabotage" him. This scenario made much more sense to LeRoy than the likelihood that he had vacuumed up the fishing line himself. Up until the day I left, LeRoy would always say, "Remember when someone broke in and sabotaged my vacuum?"

This would not be the only time LeRoy called me at odd and inconvenient hours, threatening to call the police, demanding justice for crimes that were never committed.

The phone rang at nine o'clock on a Friday night in the middle of summer. It was humid as hell, and the roommates and I had decided an hour or so earlier to have some people over, cook some food, and drink some beer. My very first beer of the night was going to be a New Glarus Spotted Cow. I had just removed it from the fridge. I popped the bottle cap with a lighter I lifted from the counter. The rest of my roommates were out on the front porch, talking to three attractive young women who happened to be neighbors we did not know existed until earlier that afternoon. No one heard the phone this time but me; no one was yelling at me to answer it. After the long day I had had, I wrestled with the idea of not answering it. But like an idiot, I answered it anyway.

"Who is this?" the familiar voice on the other end asked. "This is LeRoy."

I thought to myself, who asks "who is this" before you even say hello?

"Dan," LeRoy started right in without waiting for any confirmation whatsoever. "someone is . . . what's it called when you are played a trick on?"

"Huh?" I asked, impatiently waiting to take my first sip of my Spotted Cow after a long-ass day teaching one of Kenn's classes and then tutoring this very Christian girl who kept failing Intro because she could not comprehend Socrates's dialogues because they conflicted with the Old Testament—a conundrum I could barely discuss without getting angry with her.

"Huh?" LeRoy asked back.

"A *prank*? Did someone play a prank on you? LeRoy, what's this about, man?"

Now LeRoy was annoyed. You would get only one, maybe two, chances to confirm what he was talking about before he would tire of any sort of guessing game, become obviously annoyed, and get flustered as hell. LeRoy had little patience when it came to this sort of thing.

"*Sabotaged*?" I guessed again.

"Sheesh! Never mind!" he pissed.

LeRoy rambled a bit about his bike and asked me to come over and look at it. I informed him that it was nine o'clock at night on a Friday, that I would assuredly not be coming over, and that I would check it out in the morning.

"The police will know what to do," he said.

"Goddammit—I'll be over in twenty minutes," I told him.

I looked at my beer as if it were an attractive woman from one of my classes whom I never had a chance with but was now standing naked before me, chugged it down, and tossed the bottle in the recycling bin outside. I tried to sneak to my truck without revealing my departure, but Carl caught me.

"Dmo, where ya going?" he asked.

Expecting a mocking Carl answer, I told him, "Uh, there's a LeRoy thing. I gotta go check on him."

"Cool. Come back soon," Carl said. I was thoroughly pleased and relieved with this response.

When I showed up, LeRoy was pacing, feverishly smoking, and visibly upset.

"What's wrong, man?" I asked, not very concerned with whatever the problem might be and desperately wanting to get back to the party I had not yet been able to enjoy.

"I've been sabotaged!" LeRoy yelled angrily.

It was like hearing the sound of an animal I had never heard before, and it made me uncomfortable and nervous. I tried to figure out LeRoy's mood—while simultaneously regretting giving LeRoy the word *sabotage*, as it had turned out to be a term he used relentlessly and without any consideration whatsoever.

"What's sabotaged?" I asked.

"I don't know what it means—you told it to me."

"LeRoy, what the hell are you talking about, man?" I was impatient and confused, which only frustrated me further.

"You know, it's sabotaged—when someone does something to you."

I could see the desperation in LeRoy's winsome face, and if I did not know any better, I would have thought he was going to cry.

"LeRoy, I'm not asking you what *sabotaged* means. I'm asking you *what has been* sabotaged."

I looked at the clock. It was nine thirty now. Damn. LeRoy was standing in the kitchen, pouring a cup of coffee from his thermos. He came back to the table, slammed back into his kitchen chair, and threw his hands up in the air.

"My god*damned* bike!"

His voice was high-pitched and squeaky; he was disturbingly upset. Joking would be put on hold until I could figure out what the hell was going on. Usually, a wild setup like this from LeRoy would spiral into some great adventure where we smirked at one another the entire way until it ended in a cigarette and a mushroom Swiss burger from Rosie's. This would not be one of those scenarios.

LEROY

The list of things LeRoy cared about enough to get this worked up over was short: his cat, Sassy; his money and cigarettes, two things interchangeable in his eyes; and in this particular situation, his bike.

LeRoy rode his bike all throughout the city of La Crosse. My buddies and I would see him all the time downtown or around campus. We would stop and talk with him, and LeRoy would show us some new wires he had attached to his radio or one of his new fix-ups on his glasses or a shirt he had glued together the night before. It actually got to the point where he learned my class schedule. When I got out of class, there would be LeRoy, sitting on his bike, puffing a cigarette, waiting for me in the big courtyard, getting passed by hundreds of students, leaning back up high on his seat, wearing a tank top and jeans and a pair of oversized sunglasses he had found somewhere or another.

LeRoy rode his bike all day, every day, everywhere. He would even take it out on the highway, something we learned after the story of the hillbilly dicks who nearly ran him over. Some asshat cop pulled him over once, gave him a ticket, and told him he wasn't allowed to ride his bike on the highway—something he probably could have instilled in him without a ticket. (LeRoy respected the police very much. He thought cops were intrinsically good for some steadfast reason beyond me.) But even after the police told him not to, he continued to ride on the highway. It wasn't until those assholes opened the passenger door on him that he quit.

That was the first time I had heard of LeRoy's bike being beat up. I always thought about how nervous LeRoy must have been on that walk back to town. LeRoy was resilient—taking a beating like that, having a crime committed against him, yet still picking himself up, walking home, not bitching about his injuries or his assumed embarrassment. All he was concerned about was getting a new bike. Those shitheads shattered a small part of LeRoy's resilience that afternoon on the highway, but certainly not all of it, and the small patch that had been damaged seemed to regenerate itself rather quickly. LeRoy genuinely believed riding on the highway was plenty safe. "The police should be worried about the drivers on the highway, not me," he told me.

Leaning against the kitchen counter, but making sure not to lean on anything wet or sticky, I tiredly asked, "LeRoy, what's wrong with your bike?" As with the vacuum, I could not wait to see what the real explanation was.

LeRoy looked at me, then at the clock, then back at me, still very upset. "Do I have enough time to finish my smoke?"

I told him he did. I told him he always had time. And I reminded him we didn't have anywhere to go. Something would always hold us up, so there was no reason to ever move with haste.

LEROY

LeRoy smoked his grit down to the filter, propped himself up off his chair, and put on an itchy-looking scarf made out of what seemed to be cheap fleece he cut from a blanket or something—it was definitely cut from something larger than the scarf he had turned it into. It was sectioned off in patches of bright pinks, blues, browns, and other pastels that really did not blend well together at all. Over the colors, brown horses were running through an imaginary range. Throwing the end of the scarf over his shoulder dramatically, as if he were modeling it, he asked, "Like my scarf?"

I took a step back and crossed my arms, studying him intensely while stroking my chin. I let out a long, "*Hmmmmmmmm.*" LeRoy posed a little bit, trying to act as if he weren't. My attempt at lightening his mood was working.

"Looks good," I said. "You look like a shorter Burt Reynolds."

"Is that good?" he asked.

"Yeah, that's good, LeRoy."

Whenever I was with LeRoy and he wore this scarf, the two of us received a lot of funny looks from all sorts of different folks. Something most likely due to the fact he wore it only with his white tank top. The looks were mostly directed at LeRoy, but I would get a few here and there. They were looks that said, *you shouldn't let him wear that.* And if anyone ever asked me that question, I would simply say LeRoy was a grown man and he could wear whatever the hell he wanted.

LeRoy and his pastel-soaked horsey scarf led the way downstairs and out the service door to the back of the building, where the tenants kept bicycles. We turned the corner out back, and I finally saw what was making LeRoy so upset: both of the back tires were flat, slashed, cut purposefully; and the big white basket on the front had been ripped from the frame and was now hanging only by the zip tie LeRoy had used to fasten it. The damage made the bike completely inoperable and could not be patched up.

"Holy shit, LeRoy. I'm so sorry."

"I told you. Can we call the police?" he asked.

"It's not really a job for the police," I said. "Has this happened before?" I spoke directly but softly, treading carefully. I simultaneously wanted him to know I felt bad and to trust me so he wouldn't contact the cops.

"Yep. All the time."

I patted LeRoy on the back, and we stood there together, looking at his vandalized tricycle as if it were the smoldering remains of a burned-down house. Defeated and not knowing what I was supposed to do, I corralled him back inside, and we took the painfully slow elevator back up to the apartment. LeRoy kept asking me how he was going to get around. He asked if he could get a new bike. He asked if I could buy him a new bike. All questions I did not have an answer to. For a moment, I thought LeRoy was going to start crying again. His eyes seemed puffy and tired, and I was even further from knowing what to do than I had been minutes earlier.

LeRoy was the most upset I had ever seen him. I wanted to find who did this to him and beat them shitless. What kind of asshole would do this? The tricycle clearly looked as if it belonged to a child, at the very least. Who would do this? I told LeRoy that Pug and I would take him anywhere he needed to go, and I sat with him in the apartment for an hour, mostly in silence, smoking cigarettes while we watched TV Land.

La Crosse is a town of only sixty thousand people when the university is in session. The point is, one would have some inkling that the red bike with a white basket and an innumerable collection of wires intertwined all throughout it belonged to LeRoy or someone like LeRoy.

This would not be the last time someone fucked with LeRoy's bike. After that night, I did not make light of the bike anymore, and I listened with a heavy heart when LeRoy told me something was wrong with it. After all, he was right far more times than he was wrong. And more than anything, LeRoy needed someone to listen to him—to believe him.

I drove home and was met with shouts of "*DMO!*" when I walked into the party that had grown from a mere five people to over twenty while I was away. Nate approached me first.

"Everything all right, Dmo?"

"Someone fucked up LeRoy's bike, really bad."

"Goddammit," Nate said, feeling the same way I had when I first discovered the crime.

Nate handed me a Spotted Cow that I slammed immediately, followed by a second and a third. As I sat down on the countertop of our dirty-ass kitchen, pissed off and sad, I looked around at our filthy nook. It was funny that I was worried about LeRoy's kitchen being too dirty when it was clearly cleaner than ours.

I thought about LeRoy back up in his apartment, smoking a grit, then another and another, the only thing on his mind being what tomorrow would bring for him and his now-useless bike. I slept like shit that night, knowing there was nothing I could do to make LeRoy feel less alone and vulnerable to the whims of the slippery thugs who would do such a thing now and had done before.

I called JB the next morning and explained what had happened. She replied as she always did when something ridiculously appalling happened to LeRoy—with a short string of obscenities, followed by a sigh, followed by the silent nothingness of the gears working themselves over in her brain as she tried to think of what to do next.

"This is the second fucking time this year," she said.

It was these horrifying experiences that left my

head full of noxious pity. It was much like when he asked about buying the house across from Rosie's. I would go weeks, even months at times, forgetting about LeRoy's handicap and the very real existence of his vulnerability. Then out of the blue, something like the bike incident would happen, and it would shoot me through time, as if out of a cannon, until I crashed back to the first day I met LeRoy. I did not let his vulnerability, his limitations, escape me on purpose. It was just that he would act so goddamn normal for so long, and I would just become accustomed to this behavior. It was this that made LeRoy so remarkably special.

Now that I was back in La Crosse, my memories of LeRoy—my most distinct feelings about him—seemed more undiluted than before. It was as if I could remember him more clearly through osmosis: the source of my clearer knowledge was the surroundings where everything had taken place, regardless of how long ago.

Being back in La Crosse made me remember the events that led me to leave that place and subsequently my good friend LeRoy Buchholz. I was in a senior Phenomenology seminar with Professor Kenn Maly and we were discussing essays written by Iain Thomson, another philosophy professor who had written an abstract on a well-known phenomenologists, Martin

Heidegger. I had been asked to extrapolate on the Western definition of philosophical perfectionism, the lineage of which, according to Thomson, was derived mainly from Aristotle. Heidegger has a nifty yet heavy text called *Being and Time* that focuses on what he calls the *Dasein*, roughly translated in German as "Be-*ing*." Heidegger is notorious for making up his own words and I would go as far as to say his own philosophical language—the *Dasein* as one example.

Heidegger goes on to tell us the *Dasein*, or "Be-*ing*," and a "human being" are not coextensive. Basically, not every human being is a *Dasein* and vice versa. What does this mean exactly? It doesn't matter, and I certainly do not consider my understanding of Heidegger comprehensive enough to attempt to explain it here. However, the point I was making in class that particular afternoon was that *Dasein*, more or less, can be defined as "becoming what you are." And that particular afternoon, I was using LeRoy Buchholz as an example.

We all try to become what we are. Some philosophers believe our potential already exists in ourselves, just waiting to be plucked out of space and finally attributed to what we work at our entire lives. I argued that LeRoy (with whom some of the students in class were actually familiar, simply by seeing him around on his bike) was a very rare case in the fact that he had already conquered that idea. That is, long ago, long before I ever came into his life, LeRoy had already become what he was. LeRoy made no excuses and knew exactly who and what he was.

Now, my explanation did not go over particularly well with most of the students who argued my stance was far too subjective to have any argumentative merit. But Kenn understood what I meant. We were dismissed with the assignment of explaining whatever the hell I was trying to say in fewer than three pages.

As my fellow students scoffed at and ignored me, Kenn approached. He nodded his head fast and in immeasurable intervals as he put his arm around me and said in the way he said many things, "Good—good—good work." He paused and spoke again, "Got a cigarette for me?"

"Of course, Professor."

I gathered my things, and we walked down two flights of stairs and out into the common area by the large, nonworking stone fountain.

"So . . . I have something for you," Kenn said.

"And what do you have for me, sir?"

"I have a letter for you."

Kenn handed me an envelope with my name and the philosophy department's address. I turned it over twice before noticing the return address:

ST. JOHN'S COLLEGE
1160 Camino Cruz Blanca
Santa Fe, NM 87505

"What the hell is this?" I asked.

"Open it," he said.

I pulled out two cigarettes and turned my back to the late-spring breeze blowing through campus. The surrounding bluffs act like a natural wind tunnel to the town of La Crosse during the springtime. I lit both grits, handing one off to Kenn.

Just then, we were interrupted by a voice shouting from not that far away. "There you are! *Sheesh!*"

"This must be LeRoy," Kenn said.

"Yes. How'd you guess?" I said, smiling coyly like a shithead.

Kenn knew who LeRoy was. He had never met LeRoy, but Kenn knew of him through our various conversations concerning LeRoy and my relationship with him. When Kenn first approached me with the opportunity to be his teaching assistant, I told him I had a job working with LeRoy. Kenn asked if it would be too much to handle, to which I swiftly replied, "Of course not." I think Kenn was skeptical, but he had the tact—and faith in me—not to mention it.

"You're supposed to be done," LeRoy half-berated me through the crowd of students.

Kenn and I stepped closer to him as he leaned

up against his recently replaced bike with a radio adhered to its front with wire hangers and miscellaneous fasteners. "Slow Ride" by Foghat blared from the speakers; he turned it down the closer we got.

"What are you talking about, man?" I asked, patting him on the shoulder.

"What were you doing? I thought you were gonna be done now."

"No, LeRoy—seminars go longer," I explained.

"Oh."

Even though I had given him my class schedule, it turned out LeRoy had forgotten or mixed up the times. He had been waiting for over two hours while I had been upstairs boring and angering my seminar class with phenomenological discourse about him.

I felt terrible. "LeRoy, I told you not to wait for me anymore if I wasn't around." LeRoy just stared at me. "I'm not always going to be here, and not because you're wrong, but plans change sometimes, buddy."

"It's fine. I like waiting."

I believed him and dropped the discussion altogether. Kenn and I were now standing directly in front of LeRoy, the three of us smoking our cigarettes.

"LeRoy, this is Professor Kenneth Maly. Kenn, this is my good friend LeRoy Buchholz."

LeRoy put the cigarette he was holding to his lips and jutted out his filthy, dirt-caked hand to Kenn, who did not hesitate for a second to reciprocate the gesture.

"Mr. Buchholz, it is a pleasure to meet you."

"Hi," LeRoy said as he shook Kenn's hand vigorously.

"You keep an eye on him," Kenn said, nodding in my direction. "If he gives you any trouble, you make sure you find me and tell me, all right?"

LeRoy smiled and shook his head up and down twice in agreement.

"I wish you wouldn't have said that," I whispered to Kenn, who smiled and patted me on the back.

"Take care, you two." Kenn respectfully nodded before heading back into the building. He turned around after a few steps and pointed to my hand. "Make sure you read that letter."

LeRoy stepped off his bike seat and said, "Can we go fishing?"

"No, it's too late," I said. "But do you want to come back to my house? It's not too far away."

"Yeah, I got nothing else to do." He shrugged and began to maneuver his bike through the crowd of matriculated undergrads.

It hadn't dawned on me when I asked him, but this was a kind of a big deal—LeRoy had never been over to *my* place before. At the time, it just seemed like a natural suggestion. The two of us walked back to my house and talked about school and how LeRoy never really liked it. When we arrived, Nate was out front. He high-fived LeRoy, who rode his bike slowly up to our place.

"You wanna beer?" I asked LeRoy.

"Sure."

He followed Nate and I inside to the living room, not touching his opened beer—something I entirely expected, something he always did when he "had" a beer. As we sat down, we heard the thunderous fumbling of Carl's steps as he hurried down the stairs before he entered the living room, stopping himself by grabbing the molding around the archway between the kitchen and where we sat.

Before Carl could announce whatever was evidently so important, Nate cut in, "Hey, LeRoy, what's happening, man?"

"Bowling tomorrow. I gotta get my balls shined." LeRoy turned to me, realizing he had not told me this yet. "Dan—we gotta get my balls shined."

Carl saw this as an opportunity to wedge himself into the conversation. "Who's getting their balls shined? We're getting our balls shined tomorrow?" he teased.

"LeRoy has to shine his bowling balls before his game tomorrow. You big, big idiot," I said.

Carl ignored me completely, most likely not listening to us in the first place. He finally could tell us what he so urgently tumbled down the steps for. "You guys wouldn't believe the shit I'm reading."

"Bad?" Nate asked.

"Incredible," Carl said.

"And what would that be?" I asked him.

"Well... you guys know the whole moon landing thing?"

"As in *the* moon landing?" I asked.

"Yeah."

"Yes. We're familiar," Nate told Carl.

"The whole thing was bullshit. Complete hoax. I'm writing my thesis on it."

Nate looked at me just as I turned my head to look at him, both realizing we were in for a pretty entertaining dialogue. LeRoy was watching whatever we had on the television—uninterested and unmoved from his seat.

"Hey, Carl," Nate asked, "what the fuck are you talking about?"

"The moon landing in 1968—"

LeRoy, not breaking his gaze from the forgettable TV show, chimed in, "1969."

Carl took a step into the room, moving closer—but not aggressively closer—to the couch. "Who's this?" he asked, using the tip of his beer bottle to point at LeRoy.

"It's LeRoy, man. Don't be a dick," I told him, knowing damn well Carl knew who LeRoy was.

Carl changed his tone. "Oh, sweet! Hey, LeRoy. I'm Carl."

"Hi," LeRoy said.

"It was 1968, though," Carl corrected.

Now, sometimes I was in the mood to egg him on, and sometimes I wasn't. That day, I was.

"Hey, Carl, if you're going to claim that one of the greatest achievements in American history was a hoax, don't ya think you should you know the date?"

Carl got pissed again. "Fuck you guys. Oh shit! Can I say *fuck* in front of LeRoy?"

LeRoy stared at me.

"Don't be dumb," Nate said.

Carl shuffled through a handful of papers he had brought down to use as his defense in case one or more of us challenged his theory. "Fuck you guys. You're wrong."

There was a pause and some silence for a moment, until the silence was interrupted by the sound of more shuffling.

"Oh. Okay . . . so it was 1969," Carl agreed.

"That's what I said," LeRoy chimed in again.

Carl ignored this too, giving no credit where credit was due, and continued, "So anyway . . . this whole thing was, like, the biggest hoax in US history. These fuckers never even went to the moon."

This was enough to get LeRoy to place his attention on Carl and not on the television. "Yes, they did. I saw it. I saw it on TV. I watched it."

"I'm sorry to tell you this, LeRoy," Carl went on, "but it didn't."

"All right, Carl," I said. "Please shower us with

knowledge."

"Don't patronize me in front of LeRoy."

"I don't mind," LeRoy said.

"Look. It's fucking simple. The technology to send men to the moon was insufficient, and the Van Allen radiation belts, solar flares, and coronal mass ejections would have made the trip . . . impossible."

"Of course! The Van Allen radiation belts," I teased.

Nate joined in. "Coronal mass ejections, absolutely."

Brushing off our playing, Carl continued, "According to hoax proponents, the whole purpose of the Apollo was to distract us from the Vietnam War."

"When did you start using words like *proponents*?" Nate asked.

I attacked the wounded Carl. "Just 'cause you use words you don't understand doesn't mean you're right."

"Ugh. You dicks. It was filmed in a studio set up at NASA. They had to create the moon conditions as a training exercise for Aldrin and the other dude—"

"Neil Armstrong," LeRoy said.

Carl gave LeRoy an annoyed look. "As I was saying, they had to create the conditions for training purposes, so they just used the footage from that to stage the whole thing."

Nate stood up, passing Carl on the way into the kitchen to get a beer. "Oh, I see now. So what you're saying is . . . you're completely insane?"

"It was on TV," LeRoy said again. "Just because it was on TV doesn't mean it was . . . uh . . ." LeRoy looked at me for help. "What's it called when they take pictures to put on TV?"

"Filmed," I helped.

"Yeah, just because it was filmed doesn't mean it happened in a place where they film other stuff to put on TV. It was filmed on the moon."

"What's with this guy?" Carl said.

"We were on the moon."

"No, we weren't."

"Yup."

"Impossible."

LeRoy looked to me again, and I knew exactly what he was looking for. "Filmed," I said.

"Right. We filmed it."

"Goddammit!" Carl screeched.

Nate came back in with his beer. "He's got a good argument, Carl."

"Oh, yeah? What's that?"

"Competence."

"Sanity," I added.

"Fuck you guys." Carl stormed back up the steps, back to his room to gather more evidence of America's fake moon landing.

LeRoy turned to me and smacked my right arm. "Hey, Dan?"

"Yeah, LeRoy?"

"What's he got?"

After sitting around for a little while, LeRoy informed Nate and me he better get going. He headed outside to his beloved bike and rode back home.

And as I watched him pedal away, I didn't see LeRoy as a CHCS client but only as my friend. I wondered how he felt about me. I would never truly know, and that was all right.

Nate and I sat on the couch, and I suddenly remembered the envelope I had crammed into my pocket back on campus. I pulled it out and opened it up.

"Whaddya have there?" Nate asked.

"Not sure."

I opened the letter and read the first word: *Congratulations*. My hand trembled with excitement coated in nervousness. I hoped I wouldn't have to go to the bathroom before I read the damn thing. *We are pleased to inform you that you have been accepted into the Great Books Program at the Graduate School of St. John's College in Santa Fe, New Mexico.*

By now I had ordered and finished a mushroom Swiss burger. I watched the snow come down harder than it had all day. I checked the time on my cell phone, and I had been at Rosie's eating, writing, and smoking for over an hour and a half. I didn't know where I was staying yet, and it was getting darker, not to mention I had no idea what this snow was going to do. I paid my bill and told the girls at Rosie's how much they meant to LeRoy and to me. They were aware of LeRoy's passing and sent along their sincerest condolences.

I figured I might be able to stay at the Buddhist center, so I gave it a shot. I was welcomed with open arms. When I showed up at the door, Liz, my old roommate at the Buddhist center and the one who called me to let me know about LeRoy's death, greeted me with a smile and a hug.

She looked at me searchingly. "What are you doing here, Dmo?"

"Well, I got your message and drove back to hopefully catch LeRoy's funeral." I paused. "Did I miss it?"

Liz was quiet for a moment. Her eyes glossed over, not as if she were holding back tears, but more as if she were trying to change reality, change what had happened, change what she had to tell me.

"I'm sorry . . ." she finally said. "The memorial and the funeral were a couple days ago—not sure exactly which day. I should have told you that on the phone."

I shook my head in a sort of all around, yes-and-no circle. "No, I should have called you back, is what I should have done."

I had missed everything. It wasn't until later that it became clear I had known this was the case all along. As I thought back to the drive—if I was honest with myself—more of me than not had thought I had already missed it. And now that I was here, now that I had come to nothing, in a sense, the only real emotion I felt was failure. Complete and utter failure.

Liz ushered me inside. I sat around with my old roommates and some new faces I hadn't met before. We shared a couple of beers, and I turned down some wonderful-smelling food I was too stuffed to fit in my belly after ground beef and cheese-covered mushrooms. We talked about old times in La Crosse, the fun we had, the memories we shared, and, ultimately, the gloriousness of LeRoy. They didn't know him as well as I did, but as many people could tell you, that didn't matter. To know LeRoy for a day was to know him infinitely. I like to think he touched everyone he met, or at the very least, left a lasting impression.

I thanked Liz and told her I wasn't sure what time I'd be back but that I appreciated their couch. I said goodbye to everyone with hugs and kisses and headed out the door to meet Beth at a client's apartment. I had called CHCS from Rosie's, and they forwarded me to Beth, who was doing some admin work at one of her clients' apartments. I left all my shit in the entryway, certain everything would be there when I returned.

As I took on the snowy back roads of La Crosse toward Onalaska, my mind wandered to recall LeRoy's connection to CHCS and JB. At CHCS's twenty-four-hour-care homes, there always needs to be at least one employee in the house monitoring the safety and integrity of the house and its vulnerable residents. Usually more than one employee stays at a house at any given time, but there is always at least one. Having this job can get especially interesting during the nighttime hours. A majority of the clients exhibit increasingly bizarre behavior as the day goes one, some of which are accentuated at night. Most of the men and women sleep, but for those who don't, it can get interesting, to say the least, and at times potentially precarious.

I once heard that before JB had the head position at CHCS, she worked at these houses, dealing with that one-on-one client business. Every employee, for the most part, worked at the houses at one time or another.

I did it only once, if I may digress. For five nights in a row, I had to watch over two younger clients because the guy who usually did it was on a long-deserved vacation. One of the clients was a young boy who was timid and socially awkward and left himself open to getting picked on—he was a walking open wound. The other boy I cannot discuss much due to legal issues he had when I was at CHCS as well as a crime he had committed years before I arrived, when he was just a boy. It was especially heinous for his age, but this young man was no monster.

They were both nice enough kids, and quite honestly, they seemed to lack any real severe cognitive issues at all, outside of being your run-of-the-mill weirdoes. One was fourteen or fifteen, and the other was older. I forget what age—I may have never known at all.

I hated staying at the house. Not because of the boys—no, they were fine. I hated the house itself. It was a gigantic brown-and-white brick Victorian with a crowded screened-in porch around back, next to a dilapidated shed that held various yard tools and

LEROY

machines interspersed with the older boy's numerous paintball guns and paintballing accessories. The house was tall—too tall. It was skinny and looked as if it were built wrong. Not to mention it reeked of ghosts, both physical and emotional. I did not like it there much at all, but it was something we all had to do.

So, as the story was told to me—let me repeat that: *as the story was told to me*—JB was at a house on an overnight shift a long time ago. One of the male clients had become agitated and restless. His boisterous attitude evolved into a violent one, and he began to disrupt his room, waking up and bothering the other sleepers in the house. JB decided she needed to move this individual to a separate room, and in doing so, an altercation arose. As I was told, the individual lost his temper and became overly aggressive with JB. He pinned her either against the wall or on the bed (in what I 100 percent assume to be in an entirely nonsexual manner).

Now, the interesting thing about this particular house is that LeRoy happened to be there at the time. This was before he got his own apartment. If you have not been able to put this together yet, LeRoy slept about four hours a night. Due to this fact, LeRoy happened to be awake during JB's altercation with the restless client. So, JB, pinned against her will, was rescued by a man she was not too familiar with yet, LeRoy Buchholz. As it was told to me, LeRoy came rushing into the room and easily took control of JB's assailant, rescuing JB.

LeRoy escorted JB out of the room and down the stairs. Now, I feel it is important to educate as much as I can and inform you all that just because this client lost his temper and became disoriented, this does not mean he was a danger or a vicious person. Rather, he was having a bad day, as we all do from time to time. It's just that sometimes, with these individuals, their bad days sometimes manifest themselves differently than ours—and actually, not so differently from ours. All of CHCS's houses are completely safe environments to work in and all employees are trained thoroughly with the tools to handle a situation like JB's and situations even more dire.

It was also told to me (and easily deduced by anyone with eyes) that ever since the incident that night in the CHCS house, JB took special care of LeRoy and made it her mission to help him out as much as he had helped her. As JB started to move up, LeRoy got an apartment and was first in line to mow lawns and clean the office in Onalaska. LeRoy would listen only to JB and those JB told him to listen to.

As the years crept on and JB moved up in her role, she kept a close eye on LeRoy. Eventually, the relationship developed into something even more special and unique: LeRoy transcended the role of client and became a part of her family. JB became a matriarch of sorts to LeRoy, a role she enjoyed thoroughly and he appreciated infinitely. She welcomed him around

LEROY

her children, who knew him as Uncle LeRoy. JB cared dearly for LeRoy and LeRoy for her. There was a genuine humility that coursed through LeRoy, humility JB was aware of more than anyone else, and she admired him.

The last year I worked at CHCS, rumor was JB's husband got a job offer in Minneapolis to work in some capacity or another with the Special Olympics. JB also found herself a job out there, being as qualified as she was. The family made arrangements to move. This news was very hard for LeRoy to hear and even harder for her to give. LeRoy understood JB was leaving, but he did not have a full grasp that it meant *forever* in this particular case. The first couple months after she left La Crosse, LeRoy asked me if he could go see her. This was a weekly ritual—LeRoy asking me when JB was coming back. LeRoy's transition was hard to watch, and it pained me to revisit the situation on a daily basis.

It especially pained me because I too was making plans to leave LeRoy—and I would not be just one state over. I would be two thousand miles away, having accepted enrollment in the graduate program at St. John's in New Mexico. As I watched LeRoy deal with JB's departure, it was a daily reminder he would have to go through this all again when I broke the news of my leave—although I had no illusions that my absence would not be nearly as heartbreaking, if heartbreaking at all, for him as JB's. There was now a piece of LeRoy's heart missing. She was everything to him, whereas

LeRoy was a huge part of *my* heart, though I wasn't a part of his.

As I was nearing the end of my time at CHCS, as I have mentioned more than once, I realized I had accumulated quite a bit of knowledge about LeRoy's life. There was just so much, yet so little. Most of it came from LeRoy's mouth, but a decent amount spilled out from others' mouths during company picnics and monthly meetings. I also acquired as much information as I could from company files I glanced over from time to time while trying my best not to break any rules. To the coffer of information I had acquired over the course of some years, I would add yet another tale of yet another contributing factor to LeRoy's condition—another grand injury that befell LeRoy, an injury in the realm of the fantastic, not disappointing in its explanation.

We were driving down Highway 16, as the two of us did almost every single day, heading to mow at the house on Main Street in Onalaska. LeRoy pointed across my face, obstructing my view with his greasy-tanning-lotion forearm, leaving its schmear like an icky mustache. He pointed out my driver-side window.

"I climbed that."

He was pointing to Granddad Bluff, a very popular spot for locals and tourists in La Crosse. It was the highest point in the city at 580 feet. Once at the top, one could see all of La Crosse and far beyond, even all the way to Minnesota, literally. The viewing post at the top was contained by a chain-link fence that was strong at points and weak at others, and a large wood-and-stone warming house sat beneath a tall, epic, flapping American flag. My roommates and I would drive up the bluff often, have a cigar or a joint or two while we hung out in the woods and took advantage of the leisure the town of La Crosse and its university allotted us.

LeRoy began to tell me the story of his battle with Granddad Bluff. The time period is unclear, but as far as I can figure, and I am almost positive of this assumption, this incident took place sometime before LeRoy arrived under the watch of CHCS.

LeRoy told me he had been out walking around one morning, as he did so often, and he came across some young kids hanging out in the woods at the base of Granddad Bluff. According to LeRoy, these little "sucker bitches" dared him to climb the broadside of the bluff. LeRoy declined, but his refusal was met with the children's taunts.

LeRoy paused for a minute, lit a cigarette, and looked out the window. "They called me a 'chicken' and 'fag.'"

My stomach turned, and like some cursed soothsayer, I could see which direction this story was headed. LeRoy told me, very matter-of-factly, he was not a chicken. He did not know what a fag was, but he knew it probably wasn't good. He was going to prove himself to them. LeRoy began to ascend the 580-foot bluff.

I cannot begin to imagine how long it took him to do this, but LeRoy told me he made it about halfway up the eastern face of the rocky mass before he lost his footing. Here was LeRoy—not firing at all cylinders, with shitty hips, shittier balance, a bum leg, and near-blind vision—and he slipped and tumbled down the rock face, breaking through the trees before smashing into a pile on the ground.

LeRoy had once again found himself an injured, mangled mess: head contusions and broken bones, lying in a heap unable to breathe. A helicopter flew in to get him out of the impassable thickets. A tracheotomy had to be performed to save his life, the evidence of which you could see as a scar tissue bull's eye in the middle of his throat, right beneath his Adam's apple. LeRoy had to heal all over again because some kids dared him. With his head injury worse and his limp stiffer, LeRoy found himself far more damaged than before.

LeRoy and I were still discussing the accident when we arrived at the house on Main Street. Rob was already there, waiting for us as he worked on another new project with a ridiculous deadline. Rob overheard the end of the story as we stepped out of the Jeep. He looked up at us from his haunches (even bent over, he seemed taller than the two of us), shaking his head. He was sweaty, his hands caked in grease, and the tops of his once-white socks peeking out over his boots like manicottis with grass-green and dirt-black speckles.

"Crazy story, hey?" He stood up and said, "LeRoy the cat." Rob had said this a lot, and it wasn't until this particular day that I realized why. "You ain't ever gonna run out of lives. You'll out live us all, Buchholz."

LeRoy smiled big, ear to ear in that way he just simply could not control. "See?" he said, always assuming at least one person did not believe him.

On my way to meet Beth at the apartment building I had never been to before, I took a slight detour to LeRoy's old apartment. It didn't take long to get there from the Buddhist center, and the storm had made the roads fairly sparse. I pulled up in front of LeRoy's old place, rolled down the window, and lit a cigarette. The snow was much more intense now, and through the thick white wall, I saw my past self walking toward the door.

It was a day like every day before it. I walked the four floors up to LeRoy's apartment and knocked on his door. I was greeted in a manner that had become so familiar the last several months—a high-pitched yell from behind the door.

"Who is it!"

"It's me, pal. Open the door!"

I could hear LeRoy moving around inside: thrusting himself upward from the old recliner in front of the TV, it rocking back and forth, the bottom clunking twice and a third time against the carpet, the familiar limp stomping toward the door, him dragging himself through the kitchen with his wounded gait. I could not help but smile. It was so hard not to. I heard the metal kitchen table slam from the blunt force of a hip. A single spoon or fork clanged against the linoleum.

The door swung open, the chain lock stopping it short with a hard bang. I saw one dyed-black muttonchop and one crazy, glue-covered glasses lens peer at me through the four-inch space between the door and its steel frame.

"Who is it!" LeRoy asked again. The muttonchop receded as LeRoy's coy, boyish grin spread across his face.

"It's me. Open the door," I repeated in a most annoying voice, hoping it would coerce him into opening the door.

The door closed. I heard the chain slide out of its place as the door opened just short of instantaneously. The man behind the door gestured with his dirty hand as if he had been waiting impatiently. Apparently, I had been holding him up and wasting his time. He turned his back to me and limped over to a new chosen seat—out of convenience, I presumed—at the kitchen table.

"LeRoy, c'mon, man. We gotta go," I urged the sitting man, who stared at me with a look he gave me so often, a look that told me to chill out.

"Got time for a smoke?" he asked.

When LeRoy finished his grit, he prepared his coffee thermos and layered his skin with two, three, and four coats of Banana Boat tanning lotion. He was finally ready to go. As usual when we were together, we bypassed the stairs and opted for the slower-than-time elevator. We walked confidently across the seven feet of grass between the driveway and the street where the Jeep was parked. It was a ten minute drive to Myrick Park. When we had bocce ball practice to get to, we went through this routine every time with absolutely no deviation—there was no stopping for cigarettes, there were no errands, there were no pit stops. Period.

It was my last summer with LeRoy, and over the course of spending a few days a week with him (at the very least) for nearly two years, I thought I had seen all there was to see when it came to LeRoy. Then bocce ball season rolled around.

LeRoy participated in two Special Olympics events: bowling and bocce ball. These were also his recreational time-passers of choice. Let me touch upon bowling first.

The two of us had bowled together many times,

too many to count. I was astounded by his skill. Not only did LeRoy hands down kick my Polish ass, he was just great and made it look effortless. LeRoy took the sport very seriously. He had the shoes (black Brunswick Brunspros). He had the gloves (three pairs of black Brunswick Power Grips). He had the bag (a blue triple roller). And he had the balls (two black fifteen pounders and a twelve-pound ruby red lady).

I remember the first time I bowled with LeRoy. I had been excited as hell to see this master bowler I had heard so much about. He wanted to warm up—always had to warm up a good ten or fifteen frames before he started keeping score. I told him I did not need to warm up, so I just let him go for it. I waited, sitting on the edge of my terribly yellow lane chair, waiting for this magnificent Walter Ray Williams Jr. clone to dazzle me with his footwork.

LeRoy limped back to our lane from the ball shiner—an old, shiny-steel, soda-dispenser-chest-looking thing back by the locker rooms. LeRoy tightened his glove, then readjusted and tightened one more time before grabbing his fifteen-pound black ball from the rut. He held the ball at eye level, looked down the lane, and . . . stumble-limped haphazardly and chucked the ball down the lane with no form at all, as if he were angry at the wood for some reason or another. I was shocked—that is, until the ball landed a strike. As did the next one and the one after that. Even with no true form thanks to his idle leg and mangled hips, LeRoy bowled over 200 many times.

Then there was bocce. LeRoy and I started off rolling two days a week, except during championship season, when practice was usually upped to three days a week due to an extra session falling on a Saturday or a Sunday.

When LeRoy and I would pull up to Myrick Park, LeRoy would jump right out of the Jeep, hike up his slumping pants, and immediately limp over to help set up the field of play. LeRoy said hello to everyone he knew, and he knew everyone. He set up the courses and complained the ground was uneven or the grass was too long.

"Who's in charge of mowing this?" he would say. "I should be mowing this."

The people LeRoy played with—the people I had come to know by their first names, their preferred sodas of choice, and their favorite movies—were remarkably special. We'd see Harley. Harley walked with a stagger that huffed *I'm coming, I'm coming*, no matter if anyone was waiting on him or not. Harley was sweet in the sense that he never complained. His body was so much thinner than necessary and was not proportionate to his head, something I doubted Harley took notice of.

His politeness would have been almost sickening if it wasn't so goddamn sincere—he was just a genuinely great kid. He would walk from downtown when he was unable to get a ride from his motorcycle mom and siblings, whose names were inspired by sleek-chromed softtails. LeRoy and I gave him a ride home once; it was an enlightening experience. He rattled on about how nice everyone was and how he really did not need a ride home because he loved walking and talking to the birds and squirrels. People were calm in Harley's presence. He had a disposition that seemed to slow everything down and put even the most skittish of people at ease. His sweetness was therapeutic, and he spoke of his family in a way that made me miss my own.

We'd see Randy too, who never really spoke, or played the game, for that matter. Regardless, he was another great guy to have around. You may remember Randy from earlier, when we played the *who-has-money-for-me* game in the parking lot of the Onalaska office. Randy always wore the same T-shirt: a horizontal-lined Charlie Brown, loose around the shoulders but tighter around the belly. It was accompanied by a flimsy nylon hat, either neon red or yellow, depending on the day. Randy's hat was always cocked just slightly east or west of his nose, but it was never done on purpose. (I highly doubt it represented any gang orientation. And if it did, I suppose his hat did rest to the right more than the left, so he may have been oriented with the Gangster Disciples, yet he never wore blue and black, so I am not positive.) He smiled and clapped a lot while he sat on top of a picnic table with his feet planted on the plank below, bouncing his legs vigorously—always bouncing to the rhythm of his clapping.

LeRoy and I would converse with forty-year-old Paul. Paul called everyone "Mr. Dude" in a voice that sounded like JFK doing an impression of a 1920s Chicago gangster. Paul spouted this nomenclature while repeatedly telling us about his birthday plans, plans that always revolved around eating ButterBurgers and frozen custard at Culver's.

"Going to Culver's tonight, Mr. Dooooode. It's my birthday, ya know." He repeated this over and over again throughout the sweaty afternoon of lawn games. "Hey there, Mr. Dooooode! It's my birthday. Going to Culvers, Mr. Dooooode." He must have had eight or nine birthdays that summer.

Paul sometimes had the habit of antagonizing the shit out of the other players on the field. He would look at them through his thick glasses with the strong black headband as he cleverly stoked their agitation like a dying fire he needed to reignite in order to stay comfortable. He would push each cutting word out from behind his snaggletooth and past his lips as if some rival player had dared him to do so. Right when you thought his victim had successfully ignored him, he would strike a particular nerve and send his target into an utterly raucous fury. Paul had to leave or sit in a mock timeout during bocce practice more than once. He was a good guy, though, and his actions out on the field were just a way to have fun. He may have been a naughty cat, but he wasn't malicious, and he really enjoyed being around people. He really did want to be part of the group. He viewed any form of interaction with his fellow players as positive, and he saw any conversation as a window into friendship. If anything, I thought Paul was more than likely a bit bored most of the time and just wanted someone to interact with.

Coincidentally and awesomely, Nate and I lived across the street from Myrick Park. If Nate was not working with another client that day, he would take the minute walk over, across the park and past the electrical house, to participate in all the festivities. Nate would greet LeRoy and me with a head nod and a slap on the back. Nate would help us set up the field or take care of whatever else needed to be taken care of, but what it really came down to was bocce practice at Myrick Park was just a fucking fun place to be.

After watching the group as a whole, my eyes would stray back to LeRoy, leering, hunched at ground level, bending on knees that up until then I had assumed would not be able to support the angle at which he perched. LeRoy wore two pairs of spectacles and pushed the front pair flush against the pair closest to his face.

Once, Nate leaned into my left side and asked, "What's up with the two pairs of glasses?"

I turned to Nate, half-faced, expecting to give

an immediate and comprehensive answer. My mouth opened, but I said nothing. The only sound that came out of my mouth was a raspy moan, like a croaking frog trying to whisper. "That's a damn good question, Nate," I finally said.

When LeRoy found whatever it was he was eyeing up, he then used his left hand to grab the sunglasses hanging from his sweat-and-tanning-lotion-soaked tank top and press them against the layered spectacles, making it three pairs of rimmed lenses—all the while still holding his bocce ball in his right hand.

When it was LeRoy's turn to roll, he would toss the pallina (the little wooden ball that acted as the target for the larger ones) and wait a minute to establish his footing as he attempted to out-ground the ground.

When it came to bocce, LeRoy was a surgeon. Practice after practice, he would do the same thing: analyze the playing field, take his time, and toss the rock flawlessly. (Well, he'd almost always do the same thing. LeRoy would occasionally rocket the ball, too excited, overestimating his target by three, ten, or even twenty feet.) Each of his target throws was dialed in by those two pairs of eyeglasses covered by a pair of dark summer shades. Only LeRoy could make this look completely normal.

At every practice, Nate and I would ask each other if we had deduced any new theories on LeRoy's double and triple set of specs. And every time this came up, we could reply only with a sturdy and confidant no. Our logical deductions went on for weeks that eventually crept into months throughout the summer.

Even outside of the bocce ball calendar year, we discussed LeRoy's optical idiosyncrasy more often than not, contemplating it over Pabsts, Spotted Cows, and hand-rolled cigarettes.

"So what's up with the two pairs of glasses?" Nate would ask yet again.

"Well, it's three sometimes, if you count the sunglasses," I reminded him.

"Right. So, what's up with the three pairs of glasses?"

I obsessed over this particular habit of LeRoy's out of curiosity, frustration, or I suppose both—until one late afternoon in August when LeRoy and I were driving together. I turned down the music in the Jeep—it was either the Rolling Stones or Placebo—and I gullied up the courage to finally ask him what was up with the double and triple sets of eyeglasses.

He looked at me with confusion. "I don't know what you're talking about."

I did not receive a clear answer to the question that day or any day for a long time. Eventually, I stopped asking, never wanting to push my friend too much on anything. I always wanted LeRoy to open up to me at his own pace. I never wanted him to get the sense he was being prosecuted.

LEROY

I waited some time before I tried again. About a month or so before I left, I balled up and asked, "LeRoy . . . is there any reason why you wear two pairs of eyeglasses, plus your sunglasses over those, when you play bocce ball?"

Seated next to me in the Jeep, LeRoy took a drag of his cigarette. During his exhale, in a gesture that cemented the whole story to my memory, he said two words, "Vision eyes."

That was it. That was all I got. With the smoky exhale acting as a prefix, his answer was oddly perfect: *hssshvision eyes*. LeRoy waited a minute, took another drag, exhaled, and repeated, "Vision eyes."

Nate and I didn't bother tackling what that actually meant. I mean, we discussed it—sure. But we had to take comfort that *vision eyes* was the only answer we needed. Trying to deduce the meaning beyond it would take longer than I would ever be alive.

Sometimes when we were short a player or two, I got to play bocce too and so did Nate. LeRoy out-rolled us every time, of course. But when LeRoy missed a shot, the rage would rest in him all day. We would get into the Jeep, and he would sulk and shake his head repeatedly.

The first time, I asked him what was wrong before I started the car.

LeRoy shook his head and fidgeted awkwardly, looking around for something that wasn't there. "I played bad today," he told me.

LeRoy said this most times he played bocce ball, even when he played well. He did not repeat this mantra in an attempt to fish for compliments or anything like that. It was just that LeRoy was pretty goddamn hard on himself much of the time.

"You played magnificently, LeRoy," I said each time with the utmost sincerity, but it was usually met with no reaction whatsoever—positive or negative. After about the fifth or sixth time while driving home, my repetitive nonsense would slightly nudge him out of his funk for a little while. But it wasn't because he forgot how he played. Good or bad—no, he never forgot how he played. Following every event, game, or practice for bocce ball and bowling, LeRoy kept every single score card in his pockets, which he would then transfer to a drawer in his apartment. This drawer was in a heavy wooden end table in the living room, next to the farthest end of the couch, which was rarely sat in. The drawer barely opened due to the maximum capacity of the handwritten and printed sports scores that filled it.

I asked LeRoy once where he put *all* the scores. I mean, I knew there was no way decades' worth of paper slips could fit in there.

"I keep them for three years, and then I move them from a drawer and put them in the closet," he told me. I literally had no reason not to believe him; I certainly wasn't going to go rummaging through his closet for proof.

After practice, I sometimes took LeRoy to Rudy's for chili dogs and root beer floats. Nothing made LeRoy forget whatever he was upset about like chili dogs and floats. We sat at a picnic bench far from the parking lot and drive-in spaces, far from the other customers, because that's the way LeRoy liked it. We would take our time, in no rush at all.

Often when we were out eating somewhere, I encouraged him to try new things. He usually did not; he liked to stick to his routine. But the bocce season before I left, I took him to this little hole-in-the-wall eggroll joint, Hmong's Golden Egg Rolls on West Avenue. It was right next to campus and kitty-corner from the laundromat where I met my first real college girlfriend. I must have gotten him on a day he was feeling particularly adventurous, because he did not object to this change in venue, and shockingly, LeRoy loved the pork egg rolls the best. In LeRoy fashion, he would eat them only with his own special condiment for dipping: ketchup, mustard, and mayonnaise mixed together. He insisted I try it every time he put it together on his plate or napkin—a request I refused every single time.

Each year, LeRoy went to state for bocce ball, and each year, he made the Special Olympics finals. This had been going on long before I got there, and

I only assume it continued in my absence. I brought LeRoy to the finals, held near La Crosse, one year. I did not bring him to state because he took the bus with the other qualifying players, and I did not want to be like some sullen mother who drops her son off at the school dance while the other kids got to ride with their sixteen-year-old friend, Justin, the one with the license everyone else was jealous of, even though he was kind of a douche.

I drove out to the state match and pulled into the crowded parking lot. Special Olympics banners hung overhead as I drove at a snail's pace, avoiding the dozens and dozens of participants, friends, and family members moving across the asphalt like a slow herd of cattle. I rolled down every window—expecting it to improve my vision, even if ever so slightly, as I peered out.

Still in my Jeep, slumped behind my steering wheel like some sheepish private detective, I spotted LeRoy walking across the grass, near the entrance to the playing fields. He was walking so much faster than he usually did, his limping leg could barely keep up with the other side. A small white plastic bag bounced off his bad leg like a tether ball as he carried it as normally as he could. I assumed the bag contained some sort of playing equipment or maybe some snacks, or maybe it was a gift bag of sorts he obtained merely for participating. I squinted my eyes; I could see the

LEROY

Special Olympics logo on the bag, so it must have been a goody sack of one kind or another.

Whether out of truth or arrogance or some medium between the two, I figured my presence might make LeRoy nervous. I worried that if he saw me, it might ruin his focus and adversely affect his game, which of course he would blame on me and piss about the whole rest of the week, if not longer. I watched him shake hands with numerous passersby. I could hear them wishing him luck and him returning the well wishes. I could hear the sincerity in his voice—he genuinely meant it.

When something unimportant but distracting averted LeRoy's attention, I was able to sneak out of the parking lot and drive down the street, out of sight. I found an adjacent suburban neighborhood with a side street out of peeking distance from the field and parked the Jeep there. I slid out of the car and ran to the east corner of the fields, where a massive line of white pines stretched the length of the competition grassland.

I stood there all day, watching LeRoy roll his way into the finals through the tree line. To be accurate, I really could not technically see LeRoy playing from this vantage point that was no better than a mole's, but I heard his advancements through the PA. I grew with pride and happiness to know he was doing so well at something he loved so much. I rested at the base of the white pines during intermission and cursed my ignorance for not knowing how fucking long these events take—literally all goddamn day.

LeRoy made it to the last round of the finals but lost to some worthy opponent whose name I forget and could not find during some research (which included all of calling two people I knew who were there that day). When the award ceremony was over and LeRoy gathered his things, I crept from the low-hanging, gin-scented fingers of the white pines and approached LeRoy cautiously from his left side.

"Hey, man! You were incredible!"

"I lost," LeRoy said, dejected, sad, and the most depressed I had ever remembered seeing him.

"What are you talkin' about, brother?"

"I lost," he repeated.

The two of us walked for a minute or so in silence. His head hung low as he carried a trophy and a genuine Special Olympics silver medal, which was no achievement to scoff at. I mean, LeRoy had gotten second—and even worse—before, but those times had been less catastrophic than this. I did not understand why he was taking this so hard. He won a silver medal in bocce ball at the Special fucking Olympics.

"You were amazing, LeRoy."

"Thanks," he said.

This was the end of that. I realized this was one of those moments when I needed to take a hint from LeRoy, as I would from any other friend. I put my arm around him, and we walked through the parking lot and up to the bus.

"You drive here?" LeRoy asked me.

"Yeah."

"You been here long?"

"No, I couldn't get here 'til later," I lied. I didn't want him to know I was there. I thought it would make him more nervous, which was silly because the event was over. Regardless, I went on lying. "The lot was full, and I had to park kind of far away—not too bad, just down the street in that neighborhood." I pointed in the direction of where I hid the Jeep. "Wanna ride?"

"Yeah."

We walked right past the bus and were stopped by our good friend Paul. He stepped right in front of LeRoy, which in most instances would make LeRoy uncomfortable. I expected it to cause LeRoy to sidestep the man and ignore him completely, leaving me to mend the stomped fence and congratulate Paul on a day well done. But not today.

"Good job today, Mr. Dooooode," Paul congratulated LeRoy.

"Thanks, Paul. You too."

"We're headin' to Culver's to celebrate, Mr. Dooooode. Wanna come?"

Stopping in his tracks but not uncomfortably, LeRoy looked at me and back at Paul quickly, patted

Paul on the shoulder, then looked back at me and at Paul.

"Not today, Paul, but good job today. Good job on that bronze." The way LeRoy said it, it almost sounded regurgitated. Or maybe even learned and practiced—two things you wouldn't expect of LeRoy. I was impressed.

Paul also seemed surprised by this. Even though Paul was not on most people's intellectual level and even below LeRoy's, he knew this behavior was out of the ordinary for LeRoy. Paul backed away as if LeRoy had a terminal and contagious illness at his fingertips, but he did so in such a way that would never imply that to his bocce ball friend.

LeRoy avoided Paul's physical departure as much as possible and took a few steps with his head down, looking at the ground. I put my arm around him again, not caring if I made him uncomfortable, and pulled him in hard, just once, bouncing him off my shoulder and letting him stumble a bit.

"You did good. You did real good," I told him, now walking farther from him than usual. "Let's get some food."

LeRoy smiled even though he tried not to. He took a couple steps and veered back into our original path. He took one step in my direction and did something he had never done before: he walked closer and ran into me on purpose. He wasn't knocking me over or attempting to get me back maliciously. He was playing with me. He was being my friend again and letting me know he appreciated whatever it was I was trying to do.

"Can we go fishing tomorrow?" he asked.

"Definitely. You gonna keep one this time?"

"Nope."

I let my cigarette burn too long. I flinched so hard, I smacked my hand on the car window as I tried to bring it back into the Jeep. I felt drunk but hadn't had a drink since way earlier that morning. It took me a second to realize where I was. I blew on my fingers before lighting another cigarette. As I took my first drag, I stared through the snow again. If I didn't know any better, I could have sworn I could see myself again trotting across the street away from LeRoy's place. And I wasn't alone—LeRoy was right on my heels.

When the summer of 2004 rolled around, I had just graduated from the University of Wisconsin–La Crosse and had been rejected from all three graduate schools I had applied to. Three letters informing me in short, three-sentence paragraphs that they regretted to inform me . . . Always in fucking threes. Then there was St. John's.

Four years of college had gone by way too fast, and I was terrified and depressed to leave a place I had fallen in love with. La Crosse had become my adult home more than any other place had ever been. I did not want to leave. Not even a little bit. But I followed up on that letter from the mysterious St. John's College Kenn had handed me a couple months earlier. I had applied to the University of New Mexico in Albuquerque and had not gotten in. But as it turned out, one of the professors there had read my entrance paper on Hermann Hesse and sent it along to the admissions office at St. John's, thinking I would be a good fit there. They asked me to apply, which I did, and I was accepted a couple of weeks later.

At first, I was ecstatic, and the fears I had had about doing nothing with my philosophy degree began to subside.

My second thought was the very real reality that I would have to leave LeRoy. As you all know, I spoke to him about it over a hot dog at Rudy's, incorporating the whole book idea into the conversation as smoothly as I could, failing miserably, but getting my point across nonetheless. The first thing LeRoy asked me was if he could bike to New Mexico to see me, and I had to painfully tell him no.

LEROY

LeRoy understood I was leaving; people had left him before. In reality, people had been leaving him all his life. But I did not want to be seen as one more "nobody" who stayed for a while and took off when something better came along. I think I was more terrified of that than anything.

The last week we were together, I picked up LeRoy and brought him over to the house for only the second time in my college tenure. When he arrived, LeRoy sat himself on our couch, a little uncomfortable, but no one else was in the house, so he was fairly phlegmatic. We smoked cigarettes and I drank a beer while LeRoy sipped on a Coke. Nate walked in at one point, and LeRoy was happy to see him. He hoisted himself up off the couch and limped over to greet him, almost as if it were his own house. The three of us hung out for about an hour or so before I had to get to my going-away discussion.

"I'm not gonna see you for a while, bud," I said generically, immediately hating the way I had started this conversation. "I'm taking off soon for New Mexico."

"How far is that?" he asked me.

"It's far, man. It's pretty far. I'll be back to see you, though, as soon as I can."

"I'll see you guys next year," LeRoy said to both me and Nate with one of his colossal face-stretching grins.

The fact that he included Nate in the goodbye

roused my suspicion that he didn't really understand all this—my leaving and what it would mean in terms of me and him. I wondered if I could have prepared him better for it. I wondered if I could have prepared myself better for it. What was I expecting—some grand gesture, some overblown emotional sendoff between LeRoy and me? But then it became crystal clear: this sticky exchange was exactly what I was expecting. How could I have expected anything other than this?

The last day I saw LeRoy before I left town, my brother had flown in from Minneapolis to do the thirteen-hundred-mile drive to New Mexico with me. The two of us picked up LeRoy at his place and brought him back to the house to help us pack up the U-Haul. I had been living in the Buddhist center at that time, but some of my stuff was still back at the house. I had to pack up a couple loads down from my room and into the trailer.

"Where'd you learn how to pack?" LeRoy asked me over and over again, one hand on the back of the truck as he surveyed the trailer and shook his head dismally.

"Yeah, Dan, where'd you learn how to pack?" Jay chimed in as he high-fived LeRoy. The two had teamed up on me as if we were all brothers.

While Jay took a break and made Carl take a haul, LeRoy rearranged damn near everything in the trailer and snarked about this and that. "Whaddya need skis for in the desert, Dan?"

After a hard afternoon's work, I gave LeRoy a beer, which he opened but did not drink. After a while, I decided to take him back to his apartment to say goodbye to him one last time.

I was nervous, anxious, and unfamiliarly guilty. It all invaded me deeply, overwhelming me to the point where I no longer felt individual emotions—they had bled into one another to form one super, new, unrecognized one. I did not even know what to say, which is odd for me, since I talk so goddamn much.

I wished him luck before he got out of the car, which in retrospect felt so fucking trite and dismissive and entirely stupid, I couldn't let it end on that. I tried to save myself. "You're wonderful, LeRoy. You changed my life, man," I told him.

LeRoy stared at me for a moment, not blinking, before turning his head to look out the window. Dammit. Too emotional. I knew better. After all this time, I knew way better than to end on something touchy-feely with LeRoy fuckin' Buchholz.

"Hey, LeRoy," I said louder than I had said anything else in the last minute. I put my hand on his shoulder, and he turned back to look at me. "You don't take shit from anyone, LeRoy. You hear me? Not anyone. Not ever."

LeRoy's smile came back, but it was slightly different than before. I like to think he wasn't smiling because I cursed, but rather because he actually liked what I said.

As LeRoy got out of my Jeep for the last time ever, I handed him my cell phone number, which I had written in gigantic bold letters on a piece of notebook paper, and told him to call me anytime he wanted.

Jay and I left La Crosse the morning of June 20. Having spent four years in La Crosse, in this place that had changed my life more than any one thing ever had, I sort of thought I would never leave. That I would spend the rest of my life living next door to Pug and Carl and Nate, working at CHCS for the next twenty years, drinking Bitburger and Spotted Cow at the Bodega every weekend. In four years, even after receiving the letter from St. John's, I had never actually thought about leaving this place.

As we drove together through Iowa and the taint of America (Nebraska), LeRoy crossed my mind a few times. But it wasn't as if I were driving for hours, thinking only about LeRoy, that I had done something terrible to him. Shit, I left him with Pug—he'd be fine. Mostly, I thought about what the next two years would be like, what grad school would be like, and what the fuck the "Great Books Program" was. New Mexico sounded great to me. There seemed to be something romantic about it (probably just due to the fact that most things I didn't know much about were romantic and enticing to me).

LEROY

But then as we got closer to northern Colorado, my thoughts went right back to LeRoy when my phone rang and his number illuminated on the screen. I hate to admit this, but I don't entirely remember why he called or what we talked about. We spoke for ten minutes or so, maybe less, but the only thing I remember was what he said before hanging up: "Just making sure the number worked."

We arrived in Santa Fe around ten thirty in the morning, June 21, 2004.

During the first couple months, LeRoy called me close to every week. He asked me how to cook something once. Another time, he called to ask when Rosie's closed. (They close at 2:00 pm, by the way.) He even called once to ask if he had enough time to have a smoke before he went to the podiatrist.

I called LeRoy twice. After the second time, I decided it was not such a good idea anymore. Both times I called, LeRoy thought I was back in La Crosse, and most of our conversation consisted of me trying to explain I was not in fact in La Crosse—or Wisconsin, for that matter. These two conversations were more on the sad side than anything else. They meddled in how he thought about me logistically. The calls needed to stop in either direction. And by that winter, they did. LeRoy and I never spoke over the phone again.

My first trip back to Wisconsin was in December, fifteen days before Christmas. Carl was having a

Christmas party at his house with his then-girlfriend, Lucy. It was a tradition he was keeping up from our very well-remembered and celebrated Christmas parties at our old house. There was a tuxedo-themed party one year. Another year celebrated Austria's Krampus, Santa's evil twin who kills bad children instead of giving them coal—a true and awesome custom. And of course, there was the eggnog year when the guests could drink *only* eggnog throughout the night—and no one got sick, mind you. So Carl's Christmas party was the perfect excuse to get on a plane and fly north for the winter.

When I arrived in town—flying from Albuquerque to Milwaukee to La Crosse—Carl picked me up from the airport. Carl's house was in close proximity to the university, but it wasn't a shitty "college house" like the one we lived in three years earlier. We went back to his house for drinks and Topperstix, a cheese-covered pizza dough that was staple in our college diet. We all surprisingly got caught up with one another in a matter of an hour or so. I asked Carl if I could borrow his car to go to the Buddhist center. Volleying between excuses, I said it was to pick dumbbells, then I said skis, then I said an old mountain bike. But in fact, I needed his car to head straight over to an ex-girlfriend's house, which was a satisfying yet horrible idea. When I returned to Carl's, everything was normal and no more than five people had even noticed I had left.

LEROY

I woke up the next morning alone (as usual) on the couch and glanced around for months-gone old friends and newfound acquaintances from the night before, to which I found none. Carl had slipped off to class while I was still asleep. I pulled my legs—still sheathed in their jeans—around from their prone position and anchored them to the floor.

Lucy walked out of their bedroom to say good morning. We were good friends—her being my best friend's long-time girlfriend. Even in a disgusting green robe, she couldn't help but look pretty. Lucy asked if I wanted some breakfast, a suggestion I shook off nauseously with a slight hangover—though nothing debilitating. I seriously pondered heading back over to that ex-girlfriend's apartment, then I realized if that was something I wanted to get into again, I could do it after I saw LeRoy.

Being so close to campus, Carl's brown Honda was not necessary for him to get to class and thus was free to lend itself to me. I thanked Lucy for her more-than-generous hospitality, and she gave me a kiss on the cheek, as she often did. I went outside into the bitter Wisconsin December. I started up the Honda, a car I had driven so many times before, and made my way over to South 6th Street to see my friend whom I missed very much.

I waited inconspicuously outside the front door of LeRoy's apartment building, hoping someone would come out so I could slip in simultaneously, all the while trying not to look as if I were up to no good—again. To my delighted surprise, one of the tenants recognized me, although I could not place the face of the elderly woman looking back at me. After making me explain what I had been doing for the last five months and why I "went ahead and left LeRoy," she let me in the front door with a sweetness and ease I was not at all expecting.

I skipped the old shaky elevator, whose ominous and rusty noises I recognized immediately, and opted for the stairs. As I walked slowly up the eight flights to get to the fourth floor, the familiar, ancient smells of the occupants filled my nose. I missed it all even more than I expected. For the first time since I left La Crosse for Santa Fe that June, I wondered if I had made the right decision.

I knocked and waited. Knocked and waited. I knocked again and waited some more. There was no "Who is it!" being shouted from the other side, nor did I hear any scrapings of kitchen chairs against linoleum, any clattering of silverware falling off the table, or any jingling of key chains. LeRoy wasn't home.

I don't really recall what I did the rest of the day, but I woke up the next one more hungover than I expected to be. I brushed it off by having another beer. Hungover or not, all I really wanted was to go see if LeRoy was home, so I once again borrowed Carl's brown Honda and headed back to his apartment.

I was not much in the mood for waiting around this morning. I remembered that sometimes a couple tenants would sneak out the side door to smoke, leaving the blue door propped ajar with a piece of wood or a large rock, just enough to keep it open without it being noticed. This morning, my recollection served me well. I walked into the building through the silent and heavy blue door, making sure not to displace its secret prop. This time, I bounded up the steps to the fourth floor and sprinted down to the end of the hallway. I ran so fast. It was as if my body could not contain its excitement any longer and I had to expel it somehow, or my physical self would not be able to contain the energy any longer.

I knocked. I knocked again immediately and waited. I waited as I did the morning before. I knocked again. Nothing.

"Goddammit," I cursed the both of us.

Strangely sad, I turned around, defeated for the second day in a row. I walked back down the steps, slipped out through the blue side door, and got back into the brown Honda.

I did not know what to do or where to go. I realized at that moment—at 7:58 am while sitting on the side of the street across from LeRoy's apartment building—that I had actually come back to La Crosse to see him more than anything else. I had to leave that night; I was taking a red-eye back west. In a very brief time there in the Honda, I came to terms with the realization that I probably would never see LeRoy again.

I decided to drive over to Rosie's to get some coffee and write for a while. I parked across the street, right around where I always used to park. With my laptop in one hand, I used the other to pull open the entrance to Rosie's. I nodded at one of the waitresses, who sort of recognized me but could not place from where or when, and sat myself at a random table.

I scanned the tables a couple times. On my second look, I noticed a man with his back to me, hunched over the table with a stiff left leg protruding out. This man was smoking a cigarette and wearing a flannel shirt. Excitement rushed over me. Without even thinking, I approached my old friend—finally, after what seemed like months of searching.

"LeRoy, my man! How the hell are you?" I said as I patted him on the back, hard.

Some old dude I had never seen before turned around and looked at me in the way you would look if someone you had never seen before patted you on the shoulder and shouted out a name that wasn't yours.

I backed away, embarrassed, and with a groveling, insincere apology, I slid back into my booth. Helping to break up a few of the stares from other patrons, the waitress hurried over. I ordered a coffee and a mushroom Swiss burger before lighting up a cigarette. It was eight thirty in the morning.

I spent two hours at Rosie's that morning writing about LeRoy. I drank cup after cup of coffee and smoked nearly a pack of cigarettes. When I was finished, I got up, walked out across the street, and got back into Carl's brown Honda. I sat for a few minutes before deciding to drive over to LeRoy's place one last time. Once again, I snuck in through the blue side door; whoever had snuck out must have forgotten to take the nudge out. I did not bound up the steps this time. Instead I took them one at a time until I reached the fourth floor. I gave LeRoy's door one last knock.

"Who is it!" the excitedly high voice of LeRoy barked through from the other side. It was him—he was home.

"It's me. Open the door!" I joked, completely forgetting I had not seen the man in months.

There was no sound from the other side of the door. It was quiet. LeRoy did not recognize my voice, and he sure as hell was not going to open the door for a stranger—a label I now unwittingly bore.

"LeRoy, it's Dan . . . Dan Monroe. I used to work with you."

I heard a little familiar movement in the kitchen, and the door opened slowly, the chain keeping it from opening completely. When we saw each other, I witnessed a small light ignite in LeRoy's mysterious mind as he suddenly recognized this perfect stranger standing in front of him in the hallway. He recognized me, but I realized how slightly. LeRoy let me in.

For the next hour, I sat in his apartment, playing along as LeRoy pretended to remember me much more than he actually did. We smoked a few cigarettes, and LeRoy told me what he had been up to: the same old same old, nothing new.

We sat through more than one moment of silence, which were no longer so comfortable. Things were different. LeRoy wasn't different, and I hadn't changed very much at all, but *things* were different. A new guy was hanging out with LeRoy now. I had heard from Pug they went through two bad ones after I left, then they found a really good guy he liked. This certainly was not LeRoy's fault. But now as I sat there with him, with no real signs of the unique dynamic that had once existed between us, he really just didn't know what to do, and I understood this, regardless of how it made me feel.

When I went to leave LeRoy's apartment that early afternoon, I held back from giving him a hug. That was hard. A huge part of me felt this would be the last interaction I would have with LeRoy for a really long time—if not ever. I almost lost it and nearly went for it, but I caught myself. And in an act of truly not knowing what to do, I saluted LeRoy. It was ridiculous.

"Oh, I almost forgot . . ." I said, going back to the kitchen table. On the way to LeRoy's the first time that morning, I had stopped to get him a pack of Winstons and ended up buying him four. I had set the bag on the kitchen table when I first came in. "These are for you," I said as I handed over the four packs. LeRoy did not take them at first, so I just tossed them on the table.

"Thanks," LeRoy said, giving the packs a good once-over as he nodded again and again with satisfaction and good manners.

"Do good things, LeRoy," I told him before I walked out the door.

After I met with him and before I got on the plane home, I called Beth at CHCS and told her about my awkward encounter with LeRoy. She, being the insightful woman she is, explained how difficult it was for LeRoy to just hang out with me casually now. She reminded me that it took LeRoy a little while to get used to "Dan" not being around. He had coped with it, went through two defective replacements, and finally got placed with a guy he liked, then I came back to mix everything up. It all made sense. I was also relieved when Beth vehemently emphasized this was not my fault—I had just wanted to see my friend LeRoy. But in a precise and logically incontrovertible way, Beth told me to just let it go. If I ever came back, she said it might be best to leave LeRoy off my surprise visit list. Fair enough.

So, some seventy hours after I began my trip down Highway 25 away from Santa Fe to catch a flight, I was on a plane that flew me to Minneapolis, and from there, back to Albuquerque.

As it would turn out, I traveled back to Wisconsin half a dozen times while I lived in New Mexico. Each time I went back, I kept the promise I made to Beth—and to myself. I never went to see LeRoy again. That afternoon in the apartment, when I gave him the tobacco offering, that was the last time I ever saw LeRoy Buchholz.

When I looked at my phone, I realized I had been sitting in front of LeRoy's apartment for almost forty-five minutes. The snow had been creeping into my open car window, and my cigarette was now damp and mushy. If I had been anywhere else, I would have worried I was wasting my time. I started up the Jeep and headed out to the apartment building to meet Beth, for real this time, and I decided to take the Mississippi River bridge. Looking out over both sides of the Great River, I lost myself again.

"Why are they building another bridge?" LeRoy asked me, curiously agitated and annoyed. "I mean, they already have one—we're driving on it right now."

The bridge LeRoy was referring to was the La

Crosse Rail Bridge, a tall powder-blue swing bridge that spans the Mississippi River between La Crescent, Minnesota, and La Crosse. We had to cross this bridge in order to reach our special, reclusive bass-o'-plenty fishing spot. The bridge is actually pretty cool. Erected in 1876, it was one of the first fifteen bridges built across the Mississippi River. Plus, it makes this cool *wub wub wub wub wub* sound when you drive over the blue metal grid beneath.

LeRoy's question caused my attention to drift from our fishing trip to the bridge being erected directly parallel to us. This new bridge being constructed would eventually connect La Crosse to La Crescent, because the state or the city wanted to crown the swing bridge a regional landmark, which meant it would not be used as much, if at all. Upon explaining this to LeRoy, I got back just what I expected: a string of "That's stupid" and a series of looks that begged the question, *Why are you being such an idiot?*

My attention turned back to our impending afternoon of fishing, thanks mostly to the sound of rattling fishing poles and lures scratching against the glass of the rear windows.

"Fine—don't answer me," LeRoy said, flicking his words with sarcasm.

"Answer what? You didn't ask me anything, man."

LeRoy threatened to report me to JB for not listening to him and ignoring his questions.

"JB doesn't work here anymore, LeRoy. You know that."

"She still has a telephone, doesn't she?"

I guess he was right, technically. LeRoy held up his finger, pointing to the roof of the car, driving his index finger into the soft cloth as if it were the chest of some junior high runt and he was the bully. He shifted his body in a shimmying motion, slow at first, then much more animated in order to make sure I was looking at him. He shot a dramatic grin in my direction.

"All it takes is one phone call." LeRoy stared at me, now frozen like a gargoyle, not moving a muscle. When he felt the bit had gone on long enough, he slid back into his original position—content, satisfied, and in control.

As we came over the bridge, we had to make a fairly abrupt halt due to the cobra-line of minivans, college clunkers, and SUVs.

"We can only drive as fast as the cars in front us," LeRoy nagged me, whiplashing his gaze between the car riding our bumper and the car in front.

I actually tried to teach LeRoy how to drive once. I assumed he knew how. He operated that 1980s Montgomery Ward red riding MTD mower, which was a fucking beast, at the Main Street house in Onalaska. He drove it better than I did. He spoke of driving a couple times here and there. So one morning, early as shit after we picked up some coffee and cigarettes, I drove to this old unoccupied medical center's parking lot, threw the shifter in park, and turned the car off.

"Wanna drive?" I asked him.

LeRoy sat quietly for a minute, sucking down a grit, before getting a little jumpy, a little quick, as he nodded halfheartedly before getting out of the Jeep. "Can I smoke?"

"Yeah. Have another one now because you can't smoke while you drive—it's too dangerous."

LeRoy didn't argue for once. The thought of battling this rule didn't even seem to cross his mind. He leaned up against the Jeep, smoked his grit down to the filter, and got into the driver's seat. He acted very professional—no fucking around or being weird or uncomfortable.

"Know what to do?" I asked.

"Yeah, I've seen you."

"All right. Start it up whenever you want."

"Is this illegal?" he asked me seriously. It reminded me of something I probably asked my dad the first time he let me drive his GMC Jimmy up in the near-north country of Alexandria.

"Perfectly," I answered.

LeRoy started up the car, adjusted his mirrors, and pulled the floor shifter into drive. He drove slowly and in a straight line for about three seconds before veering off the line ever so slightly, throwing his hands up, and shaking his head no, which I took to mean he did not want to drive after all.

"Okay, press the brake and put the car in drive." I actually said it quite calmly and without alarm, which surprised even myself. But regardless of tone or pitch, it only made LeRoy more nervous. Using my logic telepathy, I could see where this whole ordeal was going, so I just put the Jeep in park, at the risk of pissing off the transmission.

LeRoy unbuckled his seat belt, got out of the car, walked around the front of the Jeep (he never walked behind a vehicle for some reason—the probability that he had been backed over one time or another was highly likely), and opened my passenger door with me still buckled in.

"You can drive," he told me through smoke.

I got out, drove us to wherever we were going that morning, and never brought it up again. I never even told Rob.

There on the bridge, the traffic finally made it through the bottleneck. I took a right down the little hidden driveway covered by willow trees; if you did not know it was there, you would miss it entirely. It's a half-dirt, half-paved road that says to stay 15 MPH and under, and it comes right up to the butt of the river. I mean, you could not pull over and take a piss on the side of the road if you wanted to—there is no side of the road. The road is a virtual tunnel with great oaks and willows creating the canopy above.

We drove slower than 15 so we could take the time to look at the amazing foliage and happy trees lining the Mississippi. After over a year of spending day after day with one another, LeRoy and I were accustomed to these awkwardly comfortable silences. They were not a signal of a stale situation. These particular quiet times on our secret fishing road were the best and the most excitedly anticipated. I watched LeRoy watch everything else. With the window rolled down and half of his upper torso out the window, he connected with something outside, as if he were a plant exchanging carbon and oxygen.

I like to believe LeRoy was at the most peace here in this place. He was a pretty relaxed guy to begin with, but he was completely different when he was fishing. It was the way he looked, the way he smiled, the way he moved. He was the most perfect version of himself here.

While driving on this little road, the last thing you expect is to end at a fairly decent-sized parking lot—but you do. We parked and unloaded our booty from the back hatch. There was my fishing pole, a custom-built rod my dad gave me for either my sixteenth or eighteenth birthday. Then there were LeRoy's rods—plural. He had three. And then there was a big fire-orange bucket full of fishing potpourri, useless to me but not to LeRoy: extra fishing line spools, a spin reel or two, what seemed like a thousand bobbers, miscellaneous lures, a beat-up stool, and of course some worms and leeches we picked up at the Kwik Trip on the way out.

Once we got out to the dock, I noticed LeRoy's demeanor changed almost entirely. He held a stronger, more confident stance. He was relaxed. He revealed no evidence of a bum hip or mangled femurs. The wind pulled his hair back slick and tight. He tied a yellow bandana around his head and lit a smoke he let hang from his lips. He looked like the Marlboro Man. He looked perfect. This is how I always picture LeRoy when I think back on our time together. LeRoy should always look like this—how he looked on the dock on that morning.

LeRoy set up his stool and in a matter of minutes positioned every single piece of equipment near and ready to his person. It was the fastest and most efficient task I had ever seen LeRoy do. He did this so he had easy access to everything, which freed him to focus only on fishing.

Even though he had the stool, LeRoy stood as much as he sat. He always set up at least two fishing poles, sometimes three, sharing the time between them equally. Each pole was just as important as the other. Most of the time, he didn't catch a goddamn thing. But LeRoy never cared about that much because every now and then, every fiftieth or one hundredth time, he would catch a really big fish, a fish he could be proud of. If he caught one of these once a year, it would keep him coming back every day.

LeRoy never kept a fish. I told him countless times I would teach him how to clean it, a suggestion that would quickly elicit a glare, letting me know he knew damn well how to clean a fish. I also told him we could take any fish back to my place and I would help him cook it, but it didn't change his mind. He said he did not keep fish because he did not want to take them from their home. He also said that if he took the fish from the water, there wouldn't be any left for fishing the next time. No matter what LeRoy's explanation, it always seemed a logical one.

Most of the days we fished, LeRoy would stay for hours and wanted me to do the same, but because of school or whatever else was going on, I could never stay that long. So, I would leave him for a few hours, sometimes three or four. Even though I knew he could handle it, I never left him longer than that, just in case something out of the ordinary happened. Maybe I would go mow a lawn because we had too much to do that week. Or I would get in an existentialism seminar or tutor a class for an hour. Every single time I came back, LeRoy would be in the same spot I had left him, glistening from the half gallon of suntan lotion he had slathered on, sitting on his stool, evenly coated to a leathery brown.

When I returned to LeRoy's dock from wherever I had been that day, I told him it was time to go. He playfully argued with me, leading to the two of us bantering back and forth, playing our mind games, trying to outsmart the other until one of us finally admitted defeat, and we packed up all our shit and carried the equipment back to the Jeep while LeRoy told me about some fictitious fish he never caught.

"You missed it, Dan. Hey, Dan . . . Dan . . . Hey, Dan!"

"I'm listening!"

"You missed it, Dan. You should have seen it." LeRoy held his hands out about four feet from one another and told me the fable of the huge fish he had caught but ultimately let go. "We need to buy a camera so I can take pictures of all the fish I catch," he said.

"A camera is a great idea," I said. "We'll go buy one next time." I said it but never did it. I regret never buying a camera for LeRoy. We never took a picture of one fish LeRoy caught.

Once a year, LeRoy went on a three-day fishing trip. They would take the group to stocked lakes or quarries teeming with bass and crappies. Every once in a while, they would go to a real lake well known for phenomenal fishing. LeRoy knew how to fish. He was a good fisherman. He caught a ton of fish on these trips.

The only reason he didn't catch much at our spot in comparison was because it was an offshoot of one of the shittiest parts of the Mississippi—literally. La Crosse's Mississippi length would be closed to swimming every other week in the summer because of a high fecal count. It was crazy. My roommates and I would go to the beach on a Friday, and the fecal count would be too high to safely get in the water. We would come back the next day, and the fecal count would be deemed safe to swim in. Even though I was no fecal-count expert, I imagined that if the level of *shit* in the water was too high one day, it could not be that much better the following day. It didn't matter anyhow. We never swam in it. Fuck that.

But LeRoy always wanted to go to that spot. That was his spot. That's where he liked to be. He said the Mississippi liked him there.

23

Through the increasingly dangerous snowpocalypse, I found the two-layered, barn-looking apartment complex where I was to meet Beth—who greeted me with a welcoming hello. She was happy to be speaking with me again, and me with her. She was eating her lunch, some kind of hot food I could not make out as its steamed from an aluminum bowl with crimped edges. I would have been handed a familiar container in New Mexico—a to-go container with Tia Sophia's huevos rancheros with green chiles and black beans. I could nearly smell the piñons of Santa Fe.

Beth stood up almost immediately, still chewing, and gave me a meaningful and deep hug. My throat choked with salty water.

"I'm so sorry, Beth."

"Me too, sweetheart," Beth half-whispered. "Me too."

I had so many questions to ask her, and from the second I sat down, Beth answered them all with a rapidity and pure consciousness that was nothing short of impressive, but that was Beth. Her thoughts were concise and collected in a way that satisfied me with every word she said. I was never left wondering. She filled me in on every little detail. That early afternoon at the apartment, Beth's words filled a huge chasm in me that had been pried open, empty with nothing but thoughts and worries about the end of LeRoy's life.

First and foremost, Beth informed me that shortly after LeRoy passed away, a memorial was held in his honor at the very place he spent most of his time: the bowling alley. The *La Crosse Tribune* covered the memorial service with an article about LeRoy and how many lives he had touched—far more than anyone could have imagined. Close to one hundred individuals came to pay their respects to the bizarre-looking fellow on the unmistakable bike.

Next, Beth began filling in the empty trenches of LeRoy's last weeks. LeRoy had been diagnosed with lung cancer in April 2006, and it quickly spread to his bones, as cancer has a brazen tendency to do. The disease infected his body with its poison, ate away at his muscles, and left him nearly fat-less—thin and skeletal—not to mention wheelchair bound.

LeRoy never cried through it all. He had never been an emotional man to begin with—a personality trait I never tried to deduce until that moment. Perhaps after watching the strong persona of Matt Dillon coming through his television set every day, LeRoy associated sadness or pain with some kind of weakness. And LeRoy, I did know, liked to think himself heroic, like his idol of the West. Whatever the reasoning, I always simply accepted it.

During LeRoy's remaining weeks, Beth asked him numerous times what he wanted them to do with his body after he no longer inhabited it. Time after time, he ignored her requests and brushed it off with the response, "I'm not gonna die." When the time came—that is, when it was known he would not be around much longer—Beth pleaded with him. She asked him *please* to tell her—if not for him, if not for CHCS, then for *her*. She wanted to be able to fulfill his very last wish.

Still frustrated with the conversation, he adamantly made it clear he did not like talking about the very end, but for Beth, he would give in. And with no second wasted in thinking about his answer, LeRoy told her he wished to be buried in a pine box and thrown in the ground. "That's how they do it on *Gunsmoke*," he told her. "That's how they do it on *Gunsmoke*." What a perfect LeRoy answer. *Fucking bravo, LeRoy. Bravo.* He also informed Beth it was important that he be buried with his mother.

So, he got his pine box and got to rest with his mother, whom he loved so much. For once, LeRoy finally got precisely what he wanted without anyone giving him a hard time. No one questioned him or doubted him or said "You can't do that." No. For once in his life, everyone listened to LeRoy Buchholz.

On his last visit to the oncologist, the doctor asked LeRoy about his pain level and how he was handling all the discomfort, giving him a pain scale of one thru ten. LeRoy responded in the most LeRoy way possible: "I have this hangnail here," he answered, pointing to his thumb, pressing it toward his doctor's face. He took turns between examining it closely himself and thrusting it back into the doctor's face. "It hurts when I bowl." *Bravo, LeRoy. Bravo.*

During his last days, LeRoy lay in bed at his apartment. When it came time to smoke, as he continued to do until he no longer had the ability to walk, he would go outside. He could no longer smoke inside, due to too many factors to list here but not limited to the green oxygen tank resting next to his bed like some cylindrical death-countdown day calendar. Todd, a real standup guy who worked at CHCS, would take LeRoy out to smoke. Rob also spent a lot of time there at the apartment, and he too would take him outside, bundled up to bear the biting Wisconsin wind and early Thanksgiving-time snow. When he was done,

LEROY

LeRoy hobbled back into the building with the use of his cane and Rob as a second, much taller crutch.

This is hard to explain, especially from someone who wasn't actually there, but something beautiful blanketed his last days, something that would resonate forever, something about the impact LeRoy had on people. So many others loved LeRoy as much as I did, probably more—people like Todd and Rob. As LeRoy lay in his bed, Rob's tall, slender frame sat at the foot of it, soothing the devitalizing situation with his positive presence. Rob would tell LeRoy bedtime stories, the subject matter of which were his infinite memories of Lah-Roy, the time they spent together, the adventures they had. When Rob wasn't sitting on the edge of LeRoy's bed, telling stories and waiting for him to fall asleep, he himself would sleep in a chair they kept in the bedroom, all night until morning—never wanting to leave his friend.

Pat, a close friend of LeRoy's, had also visited and stayed with him during his last days. Beth said LeRoy was waiting for Pat to show up so he could die. Although I knew of his existence, I had never met Pat. I literally had no idea who he was, what he was like, or what he looked like, but I certainly wish I could have met him—someone who meant so much to LeRoy.

LeRoy died at approximately 10:15 pm during the cold and snowy night of November 29, 2006.

I think about watching LeRoy's last thoughts on a projector in an old movie house. I imagine visions of bowling perfect 300s and sitting on his fishing stool, catching fish and throwing them back. I imagine his thoughts of getting another gold medal in bocce ball, coming home, hanging it on his wall, and kissing Sassy good night. I still imagine these things.

Beth told me LeRoy had undergone chemotherapy sessions. I was silent. She smiled, knowing what I was thinking. "I know. I know," she said, completely on track.

"What about his hair, Beth?" The words just slipped out of my mouth.

"I know. I know."

Once they had decided chemo was a very real possibility, they had to make sure LeRoy knew exactly what would be in store if he decided to go through with it. LeRoy was not a vain man by common social standards, but he had a very particular style and was conscious of the way he looked. He did not conform to or care about what people thought, but he cared about how he looked for *his own* sake. Part of LeRoy's signature look lay mostly in his thick, silky mane of black-dyed Burt Reynolds hair. I would have thought for sure he would not have wanted to go through with anything that would cause him to lose his hair. But Beth said LeRoy was fully aware of the repercussions of the chemo. He did not seem to mind at all about losing his hair.

When the sessions started and the dreadful side effect of hair loss began to take form, LeRoy started throwing around the idea of getting some false hair, a suggestion others warmly welcomed. Beth looked into it, and as it turned out, wigs ain't cheap. This option proved too expensive for LeRoy, CHCS, and anyone willing to help out financially. I guess I never gave much thought to how pricey someone else's hair could be.

With no hair and seemingly no options, LeRoy's friends and colleagues improvised with a hat—a hat so fitting, it was as if LeRoy had made it himself. They had found him this badass Harley-Davidson leather skullcap that fit LeRoy as if it had actually been a part of his cranium from the day he was born. The icing on the cake was that two chains ran tight along the left and right sides of the cap and connected in the back. LeRoy never took it off once he went bald.

Beth gave me pictures of LeRoy in the bed of a hotel room. She told me they were from a fishing trip during his last remaining months. The photographs pain me. I wanted to see them, but I would have rather liked to keep that last image of him waving goodbye as I pulled out of the driveway in La Crosse. He was incredibly thin—thinner than the worst images I had concocted in my head. It looked as if he were losing weight as I stared at it, as if he were getting thinner and thinner behind the glossy shine of the photograph. But even with his thinning limbs and a body receding more and more with every breath, there was a smile in every single photograph. He smiled hard and wide, very happy where he was at. And about six inches above his attenuated but smiling lips rested the Harley-Davidson black leather skullcap, chains and all. Hair or no hair, LeRoy was stylin'.

After all our talking and reminiscing, Beth handed me a cardboard coffer filled with dozens of LeRoy gems: numerous photographs from the last weeks of LeRoy's life; some meaningful-to-LeRoy knickknack crap that sat on his shelves; a beautiful, hand-carved wooden cane he used when he was out of his wheelchair; and at the bottom of all of it, the black leather Harley-Davidson chained cap. Honestly, I think the items were sort of leftovers, but I still took the entire box.

Beth apologized for not getting in touch with me for the funeral or even the fact that LeRoy had passed. "You're like a fucking nomad, sweetheart," she said. "No one really knew where you were."

In all fairness, she was not wrong. I was hard to track down for a few years. I told her not to worry about it—no hard feelings. I asked her for directions to LeRoy's grave, which she wrote down on a notecard.

"Hey, Beth . . ." I said, "do you know what happened to those coffee cans in LeRoy's closet?"

"What coffee cans?" she asked, confused.

LEROY

"LeRoy had these coffee cans full of loose change. Like, hundreds if not a thousand dollars he was saving for Rob's daughter."

"I'm sorry, sweetheart." She winced. "I never heard anything about that."

This was more than disappointing. It was devastating. I hope they got to where they were going—but the reality was probably more grave, more disgusting.

I gave Beth another painful, strong hug, said good-bye, and headed off to track down the cemetery with LeRoy's plot—the place he was resting with his mother in the quiet, rolling hills of Steven's Town, an area near Holmen, Wisconsin.

I took the treacherously slick steps down to the street two by two. It was a little after two thirty now. I looked at the map Beth gave me, covering it with my coat, attempting to protect it from the destructive moisture falling from above. I got in the Jeep and thought about stopping by Rob's place before I headed out to the bluffs where LeRoy was buried, but it was a fleeting idea I never followed through on.

When I got in the car, I got that nervous-shit feeling in my stomach again, a cross between the butterflies before a first date and when you know you're in a lot of trouble. *Why was I so goddamn nervous?* I didn't understand.

I pulled out Beth's hand-drawn map and gently

wiped away the melting snowflakes, trying not to smudge up the street names. I placed the map on my dash and pulled out, heading north toward Holmen and eventually into Stevenstown. I peered out my windshield, looking up, trying to find the sun, pale and struggling behind the gray clouds and the snow that fell softer now than it did before. I figured I had two hours left of decent light, maybe less due to the serious state of overcast.

Once you're in Holmen, the scenery changes—not dramatically, but it morphs into some place greener, some place hillier. When you're driving through this area, you can actually feel its density, like plummeting into the deep ocean without the claustrophobia. I drove up and down the lettered highways of the Holmen bluffs area for thirty unsuccessful minutes. I roamed back and forth aimlessly for another thirty minutes until it became clear I needed to ask for directions.

I pulled into a BP station, got out of the car, looked around, and took in the smell of diesel and wet pavement. The snow was tapering off, resembling something closer to rainy slush. I asked the polite Midwestern mannequin of a woman who stood behind the counter where Highway Z was and the quickest route to find it. She was sweet and helpful as she could be while dealing with someone who was utterly and hopelessly lost. She pointed directly across to the *one* street I had not driven down: Sunset. Softly calling me *hon*, she told me to take Sunset to the T in the road and to turn right. I would hit Highway Z shortly thereafter; it would be on the left.

"Thanks," I said. "Can I get a coffee too, but put it in my own mug?" I held up a yellow ceramic mug with a picture of George W. Bush with red devil horns.

"Of course, hon. I'll charge you for a small," she said.

"And a pack of Parliament Lights, please," I added.

As I filled up my coffee mug, I felt someone's piercing eyes. I looked to my left and saw two good ol' boys waiting for the coffeepot. They were none too thrilled by my George Bush = The Devil mug, the face of which was pointed directly at them. To be fair to them, it did seem as if I were directing it toward them purposefully, although I was not. I nodded and gave the two boys a friendly hello, a greeting returned by one solid stare and one disapproving head shake.

Fully offensive coffee mug in hand, I pulled out of the BP station and began to follow the lovely gas station attendant's directions, which were actually perfect. There was a cemetery called Coulee Cemetery immediately on Z. I passed it more than a few times looking for other cemeteries, and after a while, I pulled off to the side of the road in this familiarly foreign land, thinking this had to be it.

I could not find any entrance to the cemetery—it was all fence and gates. I didn't really know what to do, so I made an executive decision to jump the gate. Once I was over the ironclad barrier adorned with pointy arrows, I took a look around and did not see any footprints in the snow in any direction, none but my own. Granted, it had been snowing for quite a while, but as far as I could tell, no one had been here recently, let alone in the last couple days. It seemed to be a forgotten place. LeRoy would not have been buried here; no way could he be buried in a place that would ever be forgotten. I hopped back over the gate, kicked the snow off my shoes and pant legs, and drove on.

I remembered Beth telling me it was a quick fifteen minutes from the office. It was hard for me to imagine I could be this fucking dumb, this inept at following seemingly simple directions. I had wasted forty-five minutes getting lost, something I was in fact sort of known for.

As I drove on, the sides of the road became more and more refreshing. The road ahead of me rose and fell with the ease of a Bach concerto. There were no other cars except the occasional pickup that passed me without aggression for moving too slowly and greeted me on my left with a wave and a friendly head nod. I was definitely in the Coulee Region. I greeted the bluffs with relief and a sigh that thanked them for letting me pass through unscathed. A large triplet of pole barns sat on the top of a hill on the right.

LEROY

Up ahead, I could see smoldering ash and some pulpy material releasing smoky heat right on the road, spilling over from the ditch onto the asphalt like an overboiling pot of threatening goo. I stopped in front of it, worried it would attack my tires, until a friendly middle-aged farmer with a John Deere hat and a slight beard directed me over it with a welcoming wave of his left arm. Whatever it was, it smelled wonderful. I would later learn the mysterious substance I cautiously drove over was smoldering tree pulp. To this day, I still have not discovered an explanation for why someone would burn tree pulp. No matter, it smelled amazing and looked very cool.

I had now been driving around for well over two hours. I had felt I was reaching the point in my journey where I should probably turn around and admit I was lost, yet again. I slowed down, looking for an opening on the narrow road where I could turn around, head back the way I came, and go rest the cold night at the Buddhist center with my tail between my legs before my five-hour drive back to Lincolnwood. With no opening in sight and a large uphill grade ahead of me, I decided to press the gas and flip it at the top of the hill.

But when I reached the top, on my left, like a comforting North Star, was the church I was in search of. I took a left into a large empty parking lot and drove all the way to the very back to park. The cemetery sat about fifteen feet from the end of the lot. I turned the car off and finished my grit, dropping the filter in an empty Mountain Dew bottle lying on the passenger side floor. Even though I am not Christian—or religious, for that matter—it still felt off to me, tossing a cigarette anywhere near a church ground. I suppose it must have been my Catholic upbringing, still resonating, tugging at the shirttails of my guilt.

I was the only one taking up a parking space. It felt reserved. Or eerie. Or eerily reserved. I turned off the car and stepped out onto the asphalt that seemed too warm for any snow to stick to it. I made sure to leave all my cigarettes but one in the car, cancelling out any probability I would be smoking and littering handfuls of butts on some strangers' graves. I headed around to the back of the Jeep and popped the hatch. Rummaging through all the junk back there, I found the pair of boots I was looking for. There was a good five or six inches of snow on every surface other than asphalt. I knew that unless LeRoy's mother had a vertical headstone, I would have a helluva time finding their plot, but I laced up my Sorels and started my expedition.

Starting from the first headstone, I worked my way to the right, down, and back in classic typewriter fashion. The first headstone was not it, nor the second, nor the third, nor the twentieth, nor the thirtieth. *Goddammit.*

I stood in the middle of the football-field-sized

graveyard and lit my emergency grit. I smoked it fast, all the way down to the filter, then snuffed it out between my thumb and index finger, licked it, and put it in my front jeans pocket, the way LeRoy would have done. I thought how much easier it would be if grave plots were alphabetical—an advantage not available in this particular situation.

I explored the yard for another full thirty minutes. Nothing. I didn't know what to do. And I didn't know why, for any reason whatsoever, I had thought this was going to be easy. I pulled out my cell, dusted with ash from the cigarette I had dropped into the same pocket half an hour earlier. I held the phone up high, and to my surprise, I was getting a few bars up here. I called Beth and asked her if she knew the exact spot where LeRoy was buried.

"Hasn't LeRoy shown you a sign yet?" she asked.

What a silly thing to say, I thought as I hesitated to answer—then I realized this silly thing was actually what I had been counting on, for LeRoy to guide me to where he was.

"Sweetie, you there?" Beth asked.

"Uh, yeah. And no—LeRoy is MIA so far."

I figured I could not hold this against my friend. After all, LeRoy had a lot of ground to cover every day; the trip from Steven's Town to the La Crosse–Onalaska area isn't a quick trek, even for an ephemeral specter without his bike.

"Well . . . it's left of center, hon," she told me.

I pulled the phone slowly from my ear and looked around, surveying the area. It became clear these instructions would prove unhelpful due to the vastness of the cemetery. It was like telling a diver what he seeks is at the bottom of the lake "in the middle of somewhere."

I thanked Beth for the help and for the time she had spent with me earlier that day. She wished me luck, and we chuckled over something LeRoy had said once.

I walked cautiously over and through each plot, not finding the name Buchholz anywhere, but continuing for another thirty minutes, retracing my steps while worrying about the etiquette of walking through a cemetery. Once in college, I was out running and went through a cemetery, staying on the cement path, but a gruff older man in a Gator stopped me and berated me for the act, telling me I had no respect. It ruined my entire day.

The sun was going—and quick. I found myself back in the middle of the yard and collapsed ass first, down into the snow, willing myself not to sit on anyone's name.

Where are you, LeRoy?
Nothing.
Show me where you are, buddy.
Nothing.

I scanned the horizon, looking for something,

hoping for some sign. But no sign came to me. And as the sun set behind the pines and oaks of the bluffs, it felt as it did before I left Chicago. No matter what I did, I just could not catch up to LeRoy.

More than anything, I wanted to sit in front of his plot and talk to him, ask him how he was and let him know how many people missed him—how much I missed him. I wanted to tell him I loved him and wished I was able to see him one last time before he died. And how I had wanted to give him a big hug before I left that day in December when we sat awkwardly in his kitchen—even though he would have hated it, even though it would have made him uncomfortable. I wanted to tell him I did not mean to miss his funeral and that I hoped he understood. I wanted to tell him I was sorry. I wanted to tell him he made me the man I felt I was today.

I never did find the plot that held LeRoy's remains somewhere beneath the Wisconsin snow, tucked away in the southern bluffs of the Mississippi River Valley. I had come all that way and never found him. I felt, at the very least, I deserved to see where his body was. Though I don't know why I felt entitled to anything that had to do with LeRoy. I think I was just grappling with the fact that I needed LeRoy more than LeRoy needed me.

After so much time spent searching, it was time for me to go. LeRoy would not have approved of this at all, all this sitting around sulking, feeling sorry for myself. Too much doing nothing. Too much attention focused on him.

I walked back to the Jeep, turning around one last time just in case he was late getting back to the churchyard. Nothing.

I sat on the back bumper of the Jeep and changed from my snowy boots into my dry shoes, though still with wet socks and icy, chaffed ankles. As I pulled out of the empty parking lot and drove down the road, going back from where I came, I thought about the last time I saw LeRoy that day in his apartment. I laughed to myself. I did not cry, something I had been on the verge of doing just moments earlier.

Perhaps that was the sign I had been looking for.

ACKNOWLEDGMENTS

This story could never have been told without the love, help, and support of an amazing few:

My wife, Denise, for telling me I was a good writer day after day when I needed constant reaffirmation. For never giving me shit for the hours upon hours I spent writing every week, and for putting up with the nights of LeRoy stories told over and over. I love you—you are my favorite person. My mother for being my biggest fan since I could talk, for always being my irreplaceable sounding board, and for consistently reinforcing my belief that LeRoy's life was too important not to be shared. My father for introducing me to real literature—*Gatsby* and *Heart of Darkness*, at the early age of eight—and for encouraging me in everything I do. My brother for putting this in the right hands even when you didn't care that much about it. For teaching me how to typeset, and for cleaning up after me when what you taught me didn't stick—and, of course, for the design of this book; you're the master. To Carl,

Craig, Nate, and Pug—I can say with 100% certainty, if I hadn't met you thirteen years ago, I would not be the confident, friendship-rich man I am today. Thank you for letting me use you as I wish in this book. To Sara "Jonesy" Rust, my proofreader. You pushed me to write better when I was an entitled, cocky twenty-three-year old, and saved my ass when I desperately needed a proofreader eight years later! Amy and Wise Ink for allowing their profound name to be associated with my lowly one. Finally, to Angie, my editor; you believed in this book on a professional level when literally no one else did. Anyone this story is read by is because of you. You gave me hope after seven years and showed me how to be confident in my voice—I will be forever indebted to you.

ABOUT THE AUTHOR

D.R. Monroe grew up in the Great North and currently resides with his wife and daughter in Fort Collins, Colorado. Although he has written many things, this is his first published book.

www.ingramcontent.com/pod-product-compliance
Lightning Source LLC
Chambersburg PA
CBHW031945070426
42451CB00007BA/126